Lotta
Jansdotter simple sewing

Lotta
Jansdotter

simple sewing

**patterns and
how-to for 24 fresh
and easy projects**

projects and illustrations
by Lotta Jansdotter

photographs by Meiko Arquillos

CHRONICLE BOOKS
SAN FRANCISCO

acknowledgments

Many, many thanks to:

Felicity, for your ongoing patience and devoted attention, your splendid and diverse skills, your laughs, and for making every day at work a joy.

Elin, for your great ability with words and your moxie.

Meiko, I am elated to be working with you.

Akiko, for ironing out all the little wrinkles . . . constantly!

Kokka, for providing consistent quality of delightful fabrics.

All the lovely ladies at Chronicle Books.

My husband, Nick, for taking the road with me and for helping dreams come true!

And also to Margaret, Dee, Sara, Robert, Ayami, Robb, Elisabeth, Lily, Sofia, Linnea, Rae, Jackie, Cheryl, and Norman.

Library of Congress Cataloging-in-Publication Data available.

ISBN-13: 978-0-8118-5257-9
ISBN-10: 0-8118-5257-1

Manufactured in China

Designed by BROOKE JOHNSON

Technical writing and sewing by FELICITY MORE
Styling by LOTTA ANDERSON

Visit Lotta online at WWW.JANSDOTTER.COM

Distributed in Canada by Raincoast Books
9050 Shaughnessy Street
Vancouver, British Columbia V6P 6E5

10 9 8 7 6 5 4 3 2

Chronicle Books LLC
680 Second Street
San Francisco, California 94107

www.chroniclebooks.com

I would like to dedicate this book to my dear *mormor* Sylvia, who inspires me immensely with her knowledge, strength, and laughter. *Tack!*

TABLE OF CONTENTS

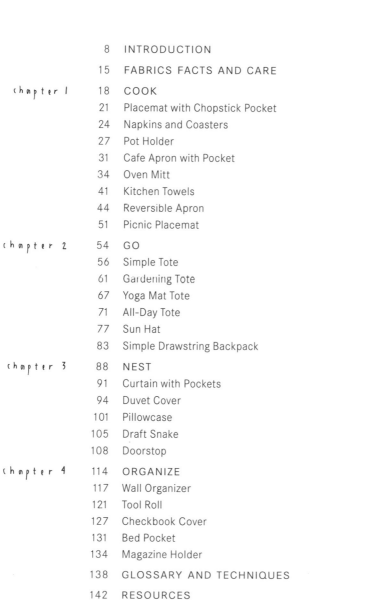

8   INTRODUCTION

15   FABRICS FACTS AND CARE

chapter 1   18   COOK

21   Placemat with Chopstick Pocket

24   Napkins and Coasters

27   Pot Holder

31   Cafe Apron with Pocket

34   Oven Mitt

41   Kitchen Towels

44   Reversible Apron

51   Picnic Placemat

chapter 2   54   GO

56   Simple Tote

61   Gardening Tote

67   Yoga Mat Tote

71   All-Day Tote

77   Sun Hat

83   Simple Drawstring Backpack

chapter 3   88   NEST

91   Curtain with Pockets

94   Duvet Cover

101   Pillowcase

105   Draft Snake

108   Doorstop

chapter 4   114   ORGANIZE

117   Wall Organizer

121   Tool Roll

127   Checkbook Cover

131   Bed Pocket

134   Magazine Holder

138   GLOSSARY AND TECHNIQUES

142   RESOURCES

144   INDEX

INTRODUCTION

For me, fabrics are completely irresistible. They are a constant source of inspiration. The textures, colors, and patterns spark my creativity—and my emotions. I am always buying fabric; out of nostalgia, confusion, or just plain greed, I buy a yard here or a scrap there. I pick up a curtain at a market while traveling, a tablecloth in a thrift store I pass by, or a piece of upholstery fabric in a fancy interior design store.

My love for fabric and my career as a textile and surface designer are a direct reflection of my history. Sweden, where I grew up, has a strong tradition in the textile arts. My grandmother taught me to never throw away material that might be useful later. There was always a place for a worn out shirt or a pair of ripped jeans. She made them into pot holders or maybe a quilt. If nothing else, they became part of a throw rug. In my grandmother's time, objects for the home were made and not bought. My mother was a more modern woman. She spent the '70s in the city and stocked up on bold, colorful prints from Marimekko and the like, which she magically transformed into curtains, pillows, and clothes.

My start with sewing came in the third grade when I learned to use a sewing machine as part of the school's curriculum. (It's no accident that the textile arts are such a part of Swedish culture!) I'll never forget the incredible sense of accomplishment I felt when I finished a drawstring bag decorated with a red strawberry. It opened a whole world to me: I could make the things I wanted exactly the way I wanted them.

Since then, I have explored sewing on my own. Never having been professionally trained as a seamstress, it has been a learning process free

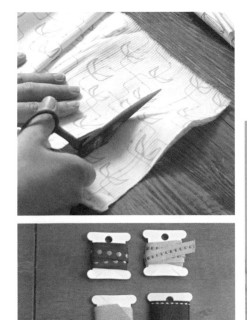

of restrictions—but also free of zippers or complicated buttonholes! I have always kept my projects simple, playful, and practical.

This book is about creating something useful and uncomplicated out of fabric. Whether you, like me, have closets full of textile treasures that you are aching to use or you'll buy your first yards today, I hope that you will be inspired to start some of these projects right away. The projects are simple with clean lines and straightforward techniques, so you'll have them done soon, even if you are new to sewing. The easiest projects (labeled **level 1**), even a beginner can complete in just a couple of hours. Others (labeled **level 2** or **3**) are a bit more complex and will take perhaps a weekend to complete. But none are beyond the skills of an adventurous novice.

The patterns and descriptions are easy to jump into; you won't have to read for hours before you start and you won't find yourself dashing all over town for obscure supplies. All of the supplies needed are readily available at fabric stores, if you don't already have them. See Basic Sewing Equipment (page 13) for the things you'll want to have on hand. If you are new to sewing or are returning to it again, you will want to take a few minutes to read through Fabrics Facts and Care (page 15) to learn the basics of fabric selection and care. If you come across a technique or term you are unfamiliar with, see the Glossary and Techniques (page 138) for a more detailed explanation.

The simplicity of the projects included here will let your own personality shine through. Let your own creativity guide you to fabrics you love, and be inventive with the combinations you choose. You will find suggestions throughout the book for ways to embellish your projects to make them truly your own. Mundane tasks like tidying up, pulling weeds, or balancing the

checkbook become more enjoyable with a lovingly made tote, towel, or organizer. Why not surround yourself, or those you love, with beautiful, handmade
things rather than run-of-the-mill store bought items?

My hope is that you will have the same feeling that I had back in third
grade—that childlike joy over creating something functional and attractive,
exactly the way *you* want it.

Lotta

BASIC SEWING EQUIPMENT

Below is a list of items that are helpful to keep on hand for the projects in the book.

assorted hand sewing needles

assorted needles for machine

assorted threads for machine

clear plastic ruler

a good pair of scissors

iron

large safety pin

masking tape

pincushion

pins

point turner (a knitting needle or chopstick also works well)

seam ripper (just in case)

sewing machine

spray bottle (to hold water for steam pressing)

tailor's chalk or fadeout fabric marker

tape measure

unsharpened pencil with an eraser on one end

yardstick

Not necessary, but can make your life easier:

assorted threads for embroidery

pinking shears

rotary cutter and mat

thimble

FABRICS FACTS AND CARE

Personally, I prefer to work with natural fibers such as cotton, linen, and wool, but using some man-made fibers and blends can be more practical and give better results for certain projects. Use what you have on hand or whatever fabrics appeal to you, it's your choice!

Because there are so many different kinds of fabrics to choose from and so many fabulous fabric sources to explore, the choices can seem daunting. But keep in mind that you can reuse old fabrics, too: used curtains, a too-small skirt, or wool from a retired coat can be given a second chance. You can find some real treasures in thrift stores, yard sales, and flea markets.

Here are some helpful tips to help you choose the best fabrics for your projects—and how to treat them once you've got them.

NATURAL FIBERS

Cotton is a natural plant fiber. It creates a fabric that is absorbent, strong, and very comfortable to wear. I recommend that you preshrink cotton fabric by washing and drying it before sewing. Use a hot iron and press it when damp.

Linen is another natural fabric made from flax fibers. It is absorbent and cool to wear, but I have to warn you: it tends to wrinkle a lot, but wrinkles of course can be part of its appeal. Linen has a very nice texture and natural feel; it gets softer and softer with every use. It can be washed in warm water or dry-cleaned. I suggest that you preshrink this fabric before sewing. Linen is often blended with other fibers to improve crease resistance and wearing qualities. Use a hot iron to press it.

Wool is another natural fiber; like its cousins, alpaca, camel, and cashmere, it is made from the fleece of animals. These fabrics are warm, soft, and wrinkle resistant. You should dry-clean wool unless it is labeled washable (which is rare). Use a press cloth and a warm iron for pressing. Woolens can be pre-shrunk by ironing with steam and a dampened press cloth.

MAN-MADE FIBERS AND BLENDS

Acrylics improve softness and warmth without adding weight. Machine wash and dry acrylic blends at low temperatures.

Nylon is a man-made fiber and adds strength. Machine wash and dry nylon blends at low temperatures.

Adding **rayon** (a man-made fiber) increases comfort and decreases static. Dry-clean or wash rayon blends according to instructions. Press with a warm iron.

Use caution when making projects that will be near the oven or heat. Because some fabrics are flammable or combustible, you should avoid them when making an oven mitt, pot holder, or similar project. Wool is safest; some synthetics are heat resistant, others melt. Cotton will burn. When in doubt, err on the side of caution.

USING DIFFERENT FABRICS IN THE SAME PROJECT

Some of the projects in this book suggest that you combine different kinds of fabric, which I very much encourage, to add different textures and visual interest. Just be sure that the fabrics you plan to combine are compatible:

- The different fabrics should require the same kind of treatment and care.

- Be sure to preshrink all your fabrics before sewing them together.

- Make certain that all the notions, ribbons, and trims are colorfast and prewashed.

- Make sure of colorfastness: you don't want colors to bleed into each other.

EMBELLISHMENTS

Adding trim, notions, and decorations to a project can be so much fun. Use buttons, ribbons, lace, or felt for accents and a personal touch. See the motifs for appliqué and embroidery included in the pocket at the front of this book and the Glossary and Techniques (pages 138–141) for more ideas on personalizing your projects. Don't hesitate to create your own motifs as well, for a more personal and unique style.

cook

placemat with chopstick pocket

LEVEL 1   These placemats will make your next dinner party unique and stylish. The little pocket for utensils is optional, of course, but adds a lot to the overall design. Do not hesitate to use two different types or colors of fabric. The placemat is a perfect beginner's project!

FABRIC *(for a set of 2)*

½ yard (44" wide) medium- to heavy-weight cotton or linen for placemats

¼ yard contrasting fabric for pockets

SUPPLIES

Yardstick

Fabric marker

Scissors

Straight pins

notes

Preshrink fabric by washing, drying, and pressing before you start.

All seams are ½" unless otherwise stated. A ½" seam allowance is included in all cutting measurements.

CONTINUED

STEP 1. cut out all pieces from the fabric

Measure and mark the dimensions below directly onto the **Wrong** side of your fabric, using a yardstick and a fabric marker. Then, using your scissors, cut out each piece, following the marked lines.

Cut 2 Placemats: 19" wide x 15" long

Cut 2 Chopstick Pockets: 2" wide x 9¾" long

STEP 2. make the placemats

On the placemat pieces, with the **Wrong** side of the fabric facing up, on one 15" side, fold over ¼" toward the center of the placemat, then press. Fold over another ¼" and press. Repeat this step on the other 15" side. Repeat on the 19" sides. Machine stitch a ³⁄₁₆" seam around all four sides, backstitching at each end. Make sure you stitch through all layers of fabric. Press. *see figure 2*

STEP 3. make the chopstick pockets

On the chopstick pocket pieces, with the **Wrong** side of the fabric facing up, on one 2" side, fold over ¼" toward the center of the holder, then press. Fold over another ½" and press. Machine stitch a ⅜" seam, making sure you stitch through all layers of fabric. On the remaining three sides, with the **Wrong** side of the fabric facing up, fold over ¼" toward the center of the pocket, then press. Fold over another ¼" and press. *see figure 3*

STEP 4. finish the placemat

With the **Right** sides facing up, pin the chopstick pocket to the placemat, placing the pocket on the right edge of the 14" side of the placemat, approximately 2" in from the side edge and ¾" up from the bottom edge. Make sure the finished, stitched edge of the pocket opens toward the top edge of the placemat. Stitch the pocket to the placemat, ⅛" from the outside edges of the pocket, down one long side, across the bottom, then up the other long side, backstitching at each end. Press. *see figure 4*

STEP 5. follow the instructions in steps 2 through 4 to make the other placemat

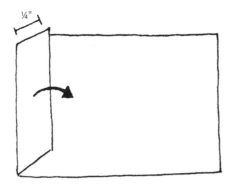

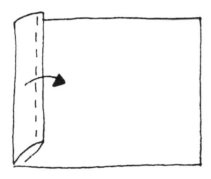

¼"

FIGURE **2**

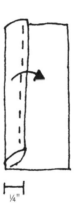

¼"

FIGURE **3**

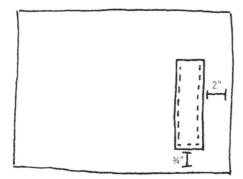

2"

¾"

FIGURE **4**

napkins

LEVEL 1 Cotton or linen napkins add a lot of practical style to any home. A matching set always works well, but mixing and matching complementary colors and patterns can be so much fun and are perfect for a hostess gift. Making a set of napkins is a perfect way to familiarize yourself with your sewing machine. It is very easy.

FABRIC *(for a set of 2 napkins)*
¾ yard (44" wide) medium-weight cotton or linen fabric

SUPPLIES
Yardstick

Fabric marker

Scissors

Straight pins

notes
Preshrink fabric by washing, drying, and pressing before you start.

All seams are ½" unless otherwise stated. A ½" seam allowance is included in all cutting measurements.

coasters

You can also make coasters using these same instructions. They're just as easy. Cheers!

Cut 2 pieces: 5½" wide x 5½" long

CONTINUED

STEP 1. cut out all pieces from the fabric

Measure and mark the dimensions below directly onto the **Wrong** side of your fabric, using a yardstick and a fabric marker. Then, using your scissors, cut out each piece, following the marked lines.

Cut 2 Napkins: 21" wide x 21" long

STEP 2. make the napkins

With the **Wrong** side of the fabric facing up, fold each edge over ¼" toward the center of the piece, then press. Fold over another ¼" and press. Machine stitch a ³⁄₁₆" seam around all four sides, backstitching at each end. Be sure you stitch through all the layers. Press. *see figure 2*

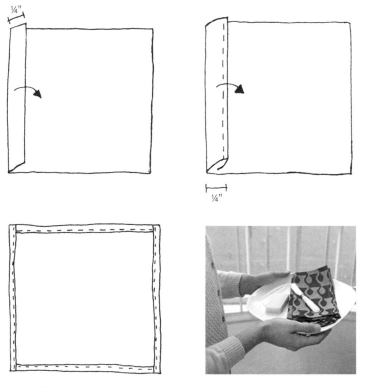

FIGURE **2**

pot holder

FINISHED SIZE: 7" WIDE X 7" LONG

LEVEL 3 A pot holder is a fun project to turn leftover pieces of fabric into something useful and nice. And since it's something everybody uses, it makes
a good gift. These instructions are for a square pot holder with a three-
paneled front, but you can also use them with the pattern we provided
for an oven-mitt-shaped variation; see the photos on the following page.
Making pot holders requires some skill because working with batting can
be a little tricky. Use a lot of pins and patience, and you will be rewarded
for taking on the challenge.

FABRICS

For the patchwork front:

1 piece 3½" wide x 3½" long

1 piece 3½" wide x 6½" long

1 piece 6½" wide x 8½" long

For the back:

1 piece 8½" wide x 8½" long

¼" yard low-loft wool batting, or 2 or
3 pieces of wool measuring 8" x 8"

¼ yard (½" wide) twill tape or ribbon

SUPPLIES

Scissors

Straight pins

Ruler

Fabric marker

Point turner

notes

Preshrink fabric by washing, drying,
and pressing before you start. Check
the package to see if the wool batting
has been preshrunk. If not, preshrink
by following the directions on the
package.

All seams are ½" unless otherwise
stated. A ½" seam allowance is
included in all cutting measurements
and is marked on the pattern pieces.

Choose natural fibers. For fire safety,
I recommend using wool fabric or wool
batting, as wool is slow burning and
self-extinguishing. You may substitute
polyester batting, but do not use cotton.

CONTINUED

STEP 1. cut out all pieces from the fabric

A. Cut out all the pot-holder pattern pieces provided in the pocket on the inside cover of this book: Pot Holder Front A, Pot Holder Front B, Pot Holder Front C, and Pot Holder Back.

B. Pin the pattern pieces to the fabric and, using your scissors, cut out each piece, following the solid cutting lines on the pattern pieces.

Cut out one each Front A, Front B, Front C, and Back from your chosen fabrics.

Cut one Back from the batting. (If you use wool pieces instead, cut 2 or 3 pieces of wool 8" wide x 8" long. Baste them together ¼" from the raw edge to keep them from shifting when sewing to the main fabric pieces.)

Cut one 5" piece from the twill tape.

STEP 2. make the patchwork front of the pot holder

A. With the **Right** sides together, place Front B and Front C together, matching up the raw edges on one short side. Machine stitch a ½" seam along the matched raw edges, backstitching at each end. Press the seam allowance open.

B. With the **Right** sides together, place Front A and Front B/C, matching up the long-side raw edges. Stitch a ½" seam along the matched raw edges. Press the seam allowance open. The front is now complete.

STEP 3. assemble the pot holder

A. Layer the front, back, and batting in the following order: front **Right** side facing up, back **Right** side facing down, then the batting. Match all raw edges. Make a loop in the twill tape or ribbon, lining up the cut ends. Place the loop in one corner, between the front and back layers with the loop facing inside toward the center of the pot holder. *see figure 3A*

B. Pin the layers together. Stitch a ½" seam around the pot holder, leaving a 3" opening centered on one side, backstitching at each end. Using your scissors, trim the corners at a 45-degree angle to reduce the bulk. Make sure you do not clip into your stitching. *see figure 3B*

C. Turn the pot holder **Right**-side out, holding the Back and the batting together as one piece. Use a point turner to push out the corners. (See page 141 for an explanation of a point turner.)

STEP 4. finish the pot holder

Press the edges flat, making sure to enclose the raw edges of the opening. Pin the opening closed. Then topstitch around all sides, ¼" in from the finished edges. Make sure you stitch through all layers. (See page 141 for an explanation of topstitching.)

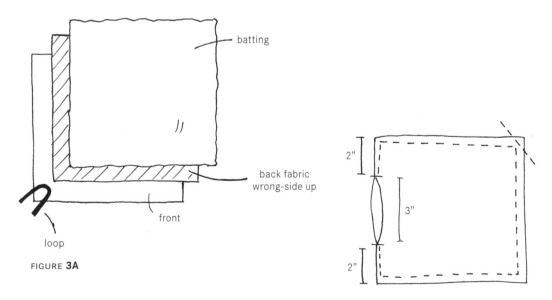

FIGURE **3A**

FIGURE **3B**

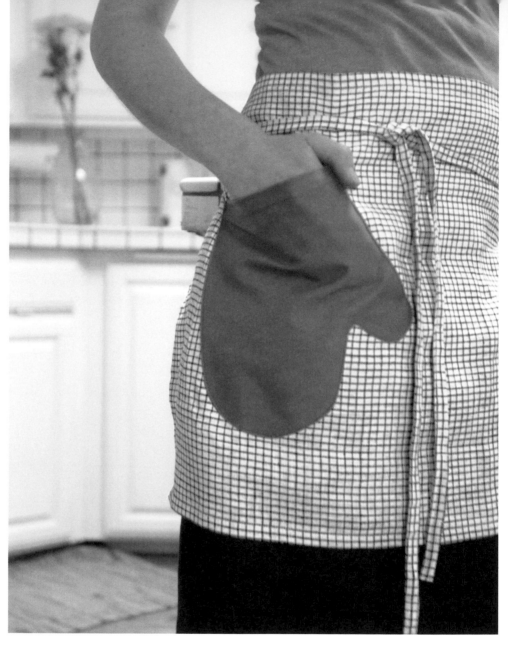

cafe apron with pocket

FINISHED SIZE: 17" WIDE X 37" LONG

LEVEL 2 This apron fits everyone and is very comfortable and practical, plus the oven mitt–shaped pocket adds a little humor to the design. But consider adding your own embellishments: omit the pocket and add decorations instead. The cafe apron is fun to customize for him or her, a particular friend, or a specific season. Be inspired by the fabric or an upcoming event. With or without a pocket, it is a very easy project that suits all skill levels.

FABRICS

1 yard (44" wide) medium-weight cotton or linen for the apron

½ yard (44" wide) matching or contrasting medium-weight cotton or linen for the pocket

SUPPLIES

Scissors

Straight pins

Yardstick or ruler

Fabric marker

notes

Preshrink fabric by washing, drying, and pressing before you start.

All seams are ½" unless otherwise stated. A ½" seam allowance is included in all cutting measurements and is marked on the pattern pieces.

CONTINUED

STEP 1. cut out all pieces from the fabric

A. Cut out the Cafe Apron Pocket pattern piece provided in the pocket on the inside cover of this book.

B. Pin the pattern piece to the fabric you chose for your pocket and, using your scissors, cut out the piece, following the solid cutting lines on the pattern piece.

C. Measure and mark the dimensions below directly onto the **Wrong** side of your apron fabric, using a yardstick and a fabric marker. Then, using your scissors, cut out each piece, following the marked lines.

Cut 1 Apron: 38" wide x 19" tall

Cut 2 Ties: 2" wide x 36" long

STEP 2. sew the apron

A. On both short sides of the apron, fold under ½" and press, then fold under another ½" and press. On one long side, fold under ½" and press, then fold under another ½" and press. Stitch around these three sides at a ⅜" seam allowance, making sure to catch all layers, and backstitching at beginning and end to secure. On long top edge, fold under ½" and press, then fold under another ½" and press. Set aside.

B. To make ties, fold under ½" of one short end of tie and press. Trim diagonally to the corners. Fold in each long edge inward to meet in the center, press. Then fold the tie in half lengthwise and press again to create a tie ½" wide with four layers of fabric. Stitch along the long open edge, and down the short folded under end. Do the same for the other tie.

C. To attach the ties to the apron, tuck the unfinished end of each tie under the folded top edge of the apron and pin in place. Stitch the ties in place while stitching the top edge hem by following the stitching line on one side-seam toward the top edge, across the top and down the opposite side edge. Stitch across the apron, securing the folded hem ⅜" from the top edge. To reinforce the edges and secure the ties, stitch over the side and top seams a second time. *see figure 2C*

STEP 3. make the pocket

A. Fold over the top edge of the pocket ¼" toward the **Wrong** side, press, fold over another ½" and press. Stitch down using a ⅜" seam allowance.

B. Fold over the remaining three edges ¼" toward the **Wrong** side, clipping the curved seam allowance so that it lays flat. Make sure you do not clip more than ⅛" into the seam allowance. Press. *see figure 3B*

C. Try on the apron and decide where you want to place the pocket and pin it in place. Stitch the pocket onto the apron close to the edge, backstitching at each end. *see figure 3C*

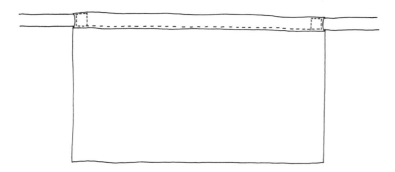

FIGURE **2C**

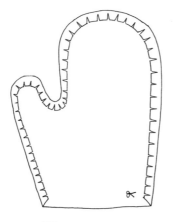

FIGURE **3B**

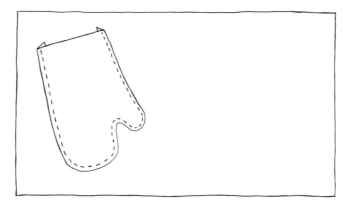

FIGURE **3C**

oven mitt

FINISHED SIZE: 7" WIDE X 11.5" LONG

LEVEL 3

This project is really fun to try, especially if you play around with the decorative stitching and make some crazy patterns. Match or mismatch fabrics—that's your choice. This oven mitt is a bit more challenging to make than the pot holder since you are now sewing the batting in a pattern, not just stitching the edges. This is a great way to learn quilting basics, so take your time and have fun!

FABRICS

⅜ yard (44" wide) medium-weight cotton for the mitt front and back

⅜ yard (44" wide) coordinating medium-weight cotton for the lining

Fabric piece for binding the edge of the mitt (at least 3" x 13")

½" yard high-loft wool batting, or three 10" x 14" pieces of wool fabric

SUPPLIES

Scissors

Yardstick

Fabric marker

Straight pins

Ruler

Hand sewing needle and thread

notes

Preshrink fabric by washing, drying, and pressing before you start. Check the package to see if the wool batting has been preshrunk. If not, preshrink by following the directions on the package.

All seams are ½" unless otherwise stated. A ½" seam allowance is included in all cutting measurements and is marked on the pattern pieces.

For fire safety reasons, I recommend using wool fabric or wool batting, as wool is slow burning and self-extinguishing. If you cannot find wool batting, and don't have wool pieces, substitute polyester batting. Cotton is not recommended.

CONTINUED

STEP 1. cut out all pieces from the fabric

A. Cut out the Oven Mitt pattern piece provided in the pocket on the inside cover of this book. Set aside.

B. Measure and mark the dimensions below directly onto the **Wrong** side of your fabric, using a yardstick and a fabric marker. Then, using your scissors, cut out each piece, following the marked lines.

From the fabric for the front and back:
Cut 2 pieces: 11" wide x 14" long

From the fabric for the mitt lining:
Cut 2 pieces: 11" wide x 14" long

From the batting:
Cut 2 pieces: 11" wide x 14" long

(If you use wool pieces instead, cut 4 to 6 pieces of wool 11" wide x 14" long. Baste 2 or 3 pieces for each side of the mitt together ¼" from the raw edge to keep them from shifting when sewing to the main fabric pieces.)

STEP 2. quilt the front and back of the oven mitt

A. In the following order, make a "quilted sandwich":

Place one piece of the lining with the **Wrong** side facing up. Place one piece of the batting on top. Then place one piece of the outside fabric with the **Right** side facing up. Match up the raw edges all around. Repeat to make the second sandwich.

B. Working from the middle of one quilted sandwich to the outer edges, machine stitch the layers together with a fairly long stitch length. You can be creative and quilt any design you like—spirals, concentric circles, or random squiggles. Make sure you keep the batting from shifting outside the edges of the two pieces of fabric. Repeat this step with the second sandwich. *see figure 2A+B*

STEP 3. make the oven mitt

A. Pin the mitt pattern piece to a quilted sandwich. Trace the outline on your quilted sandwich, following the solid cutting lines on the pattern piece. Use your scissors to cut out the piece. Repeat the step with the second sandwich, making sure it is the mirror image of the other. You will now have a mitt front and a mitt back. *see figure 3A*

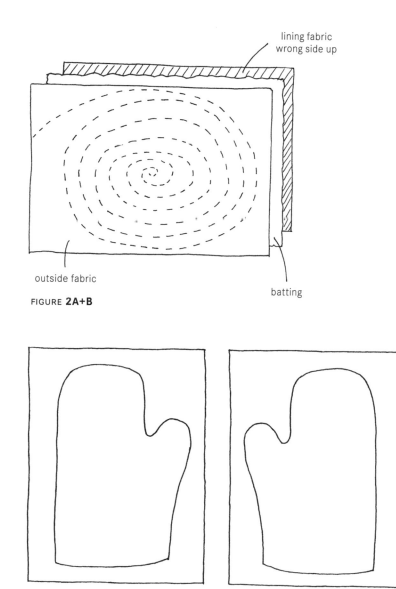

lining fabric
wrong side up

outside fabric

batting

FIGURE **2A+B**

piece 1

piece 2

FIGURE **3A**

CONTINUED

B. With the **Right** sides together, pin the mitt front and back together, matching up the raw edges. Stitch a ½" seam along the long outside edges, backstitching at each end. Do not stitch the short end of the mitt. Next, using your scissors, clip into your seam allowance around the outside curves so that when the lining is turned to the inside the curve will be smooth. Make sure you do not clip into the stitching. Press the seam allowance open at each end. Turn the mitt so that the lining is inside. Set aside. *see figure 3B*

STEP 4. finish the oven mitt

A. Using a ruler and a fabric marker, measure and mark a 2" x 12" rectangle directly onto the **Wrong** side of your binding fabric. Then, using your scissors cut out the binding piece, following the marked lines.

B. Fold each long edge inward to meet in the center. Press. Fold the binding in half lengthwise and press again. *see figure 4B*

C. Sandwich the binding around the raw open edge of the oven mitt and pin in place. Fold the ending edge under ½" so that the raw edge is tucked in. Using the hand sewing needle and thread, topstitch in place using a ⅜" seam allowance, making sure you stitch through all layers. (See page 141 for an explanation of topstitching.)

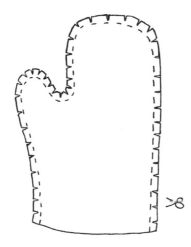

FIGURE **3B**

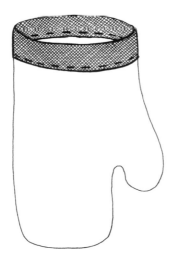

FIGURE **4B**

kitchen towels

LEVEL 1

Cloth towels are so much prettier than paper towels and, when well chosen, add a sense of coherent style to your home. They are so simple to make, you can create many different variations and styles by adding extra accents with embroidery and other embellishments. Dress your kitchen for any occasion. This is a very easy project that will take less than an hour to complete even for beginners.

FABRICS *(for a set of 2 towels)*

¾ yard (44" wide) light-weight cotton or linen for the towels

¼ yard (½" wide) twill tape or cotton ribbon for the towel loops

SUPPLIES

Yardstick

Fabric marker

Scissors

Straight pins

notes

Preshrink by washing, drying, and pressing before you start.

All seams are ½" unless otherwise stated. A ½" seam allowance is included in all cutting measurements.

CONTINUED

STEP 1. cut out all pieces from the fabric

Measure and mark the dimensions below directly onto the **Wrong** side of your fabric, using a yardstick and a fabric marker. Then, using your scissors, cut out each piece, following the marked lines.

From the fabric: Cut 2 Towels: 18" wide x 24" long

From the twill tape: Cut 2 Loops: 4½" long

STEP 2. make the towels

A. With the **Wrong** side of the fabric facing up, fold each edge over ¼" toward center of the towel, then press. Fold over another ¼" and press. Set aside.

B. Fold the twill tape so it makes a loop, and tuck it under the fold in the center of one short side. Pin the loop in place.

C. Machine stitch a ³⁄₁₆" seam around all four sides, backstitching at each end. Make sure you stitch through all the layers. Press. *see figure 2C*

D. With the **Right** side up, stitch across the loop, just inside the folded edge (approximately ¹⁄₁₆ to ⅛"), through all the layers. This will stop the edge from curling. *see figure 2D*

STEP 3. repeat steps 1 and 2 to make the second towel

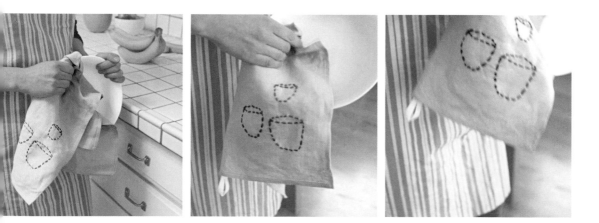

FIGURE **2C**

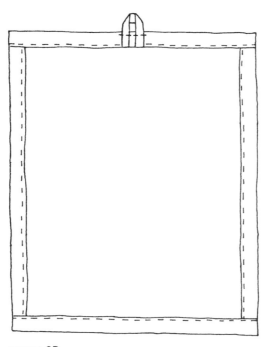

FIGURE **2D**

reversible apron

LEVEL 4 This apron goes well beyond the kitchen. It fits well and, in a fabric you love, you'll be tempted to wear it with your favorite jeans on Saturday night! The best thing about it is that you can flip it over to hide splatters—no need to worry about spilling sauce just as the doorbell rings. The reversible apron project requires some sewing experience. Allow a day or so to finish it, especially if you want to decorate it with some appliqué.

FABRICS

1 yard (44" wide) light-weight cotton print

1 yard (44" wide) light-weight cotton coordinating solid

SUPPLIES

Scissors

Straight pins

Fabric marker

Yardstick

Unsharpened pencil with an eraser on one end

Point turner

Hand sewing needle and thread

notes

Preshrink by washing, drying, and pressing before you start.

All seams are ½" unless otherwise stated. A ½" seam allowance is included in all cutting measurements and is marked on the pattern pieces.

CONTINUED

STEP 1. cut out all pieces from the fabric

A. Cut out the Reversible Apron pattern pieces provided in the pocket on the inside cover of this book: Reversible Apron Center Panel and Side Panel.

B. With the **Right** sides together fold the print fabric in half lengthwise, matching up the raw edges. Pin the pattern pieces to the fabric, making sure you align the grain line marked on the pattern with the grain of the fabric. Using your scissors, cut out each piece, following the solid cutting lines on the pattern pieces. You will have 1 center panel and 2 side panels. Using a fabric marker, transfer notch markings (for pleats and location of side apron strings) from the patterns to each fabric piece by making ¼" clips into the seam allowances of the fabric pieces. Unless you are using a fadeout fabric marker, make sure your markings are within the ½" seam allowance. Repeat with the solid fabric. (See page 139 for an explanation of grain.)

C. Cut out the apron strings from the two fabrics. Measure and mark the dimensions below directly onto the **Wrong** side of the fabrics, using a yardstick and a fabric marker. Then, using your scissors, cut out each piece, following the marked lines.

4 strips of each fabric: 1½" wide x 25" long

STEP 2. sew the apron

A. Make the apron strings. With the **Right** sides together, pin one print fabric strip to one solid fabric strip, matching up the raw edges. Machine stitch a ¼" seam down one long edge, across the short edge and up the other long edge, leaving one short end open. Using your scissors, trim the corners at the short end of the string at a 45-degree angle to reduce the bulk. Turn the strings right-side out and press. Turning apron strings can be a little tricky. An easy way is to push the eraser end of a pencil into the tube you've created, starting at the seam on the short end. As you keep pushing the pencil toward the opening at the other end of the string, the fabric will gather on the pencil. When you reach the opening the pencil will emerge and you can pull the stitched end out. Press flat. Repeat with the remaining fabric strips. You will have four apron strings. Set aside.

CONTINUED

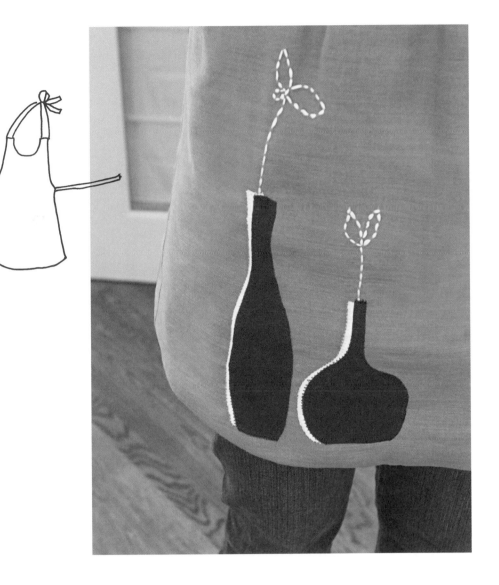

B. Make the body of the apron. With the **Right** sides together, pin the two print fabric side panels to the print center panel, matching up the notches. Machine stitch the side seams, backstitching at each end. Repeat with the pieces cut from the solid fabric.

C. On the print fabric apron center panel, make two pleats on the top edge (located between the neckline and the armholes) by folding the fabric toward the neckline, matching up the notches, and pinning. Each pleat will be ¼" wide. Machine stitch the pleats in place, ¼" in from the raw edge. Repeat with the solid fabric. If you wish to add appliqués or other embellishments on the solid-colored side of the apron, do so now before you sew the two sides together. *see figure 2C*

D. With the **Right** sides together, match up the raw edges of the apron strings with the raw edges of the print fabric on the two apron side panels, following the placement markings. The print side of the apron string should be down, the solid side should be facing up. Pin, then baste the strings in place, ¼" in from the raw edges. (See page 138 for an explanation of basting.)

E. With the **Right** sides together, place the other two apron strings on top of the pleats on each side of the neckline, matching up the raw edges. Pin, then baste the strings in place, ¼" in from the raw edges.

F. With the **Right** sides together, pin the two apron pieces, sandwiching the straps inside. Using a ½" seam, stitch around all the sides, leaving a 6" opening along the bottom and backstitching at each end. (See page 138 for an explanation of backstitching.)

G. Using your scissors, trim the corners at a 45-degree angle to reduce the bulk, and clip the curved seams at the neckline, side seams, and bottom edge so they lay flat. Make sure you do not clip into your stitching. *see figure 2G*

H. Turn the apron **Right**-side out. Push out the corners with a point turner. To enclose the raw edges at the opening, fold the raw edges under ½" and pin the opening closed. Press. Slip stitch the opening closed with the hand sewing needle and thread. If you prefer, edge stitch the opening closed by machine. Press. (See page 141 for an explanation of slip stitching.)

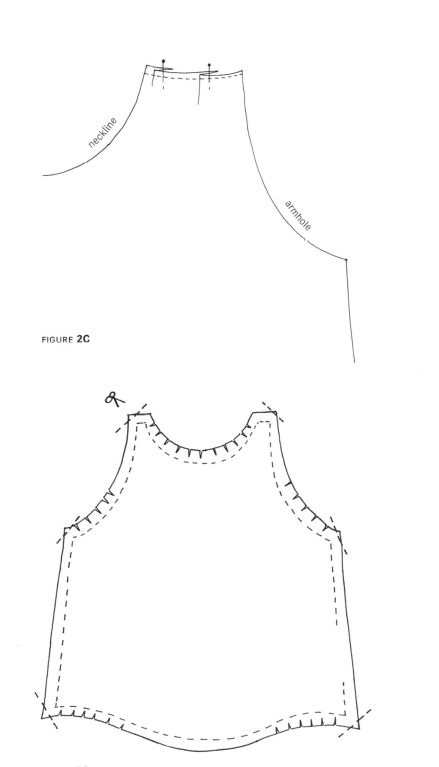

neckline

armhole

FIGURE **2C**

FIGURE **2G**

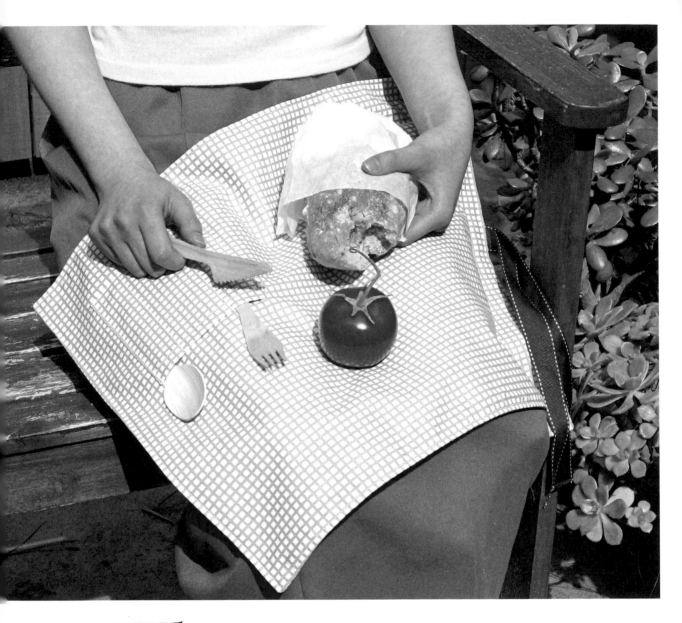

picnic placemat

FINISHED SIZE: 2 PLACEMATS, EACH 20" WIDE X 15" TALL

LEVEL 2

Here is a placemat and cutlery holder all in one—very practical when dining alfresco. It rolls up for easy storing and transportation, and will add a degree of chic to your picnic routine. It's the perfect gift for friends who seem to have everything. The picnic placemat is a good project to start with if you are still getting to know your sewing machine. It is easy and quick to complete.

FABRICS *(for a set of 2 mats)*

1⅞ yards (44" wide) medium- to heavy-weight cotton or linen fabric

¾ yard (1" wide) ribbon

SUPPLIES

Yardstick

Fabric marker

Scissors

Straight pins

Ruler

Fadeout fabric marker (or tailor's chalk)

Point turner

notes

Preshrink fabric by washing, drying, and pressing before you start.

All seams are ½" unless otherwise stated. A ½" seam allowance is included in all cutting measurements.

CONTINUED

STEP 1. cut out all pieces from the fabric

Measure and mark the dimensions below directly onto the **Wrong** side of your fabric, using a yardstick and a fabric marker. Then, using your scissors, cut out each piece, following the marked lines.

Cut 4 Placemats (2 fronts and 2 linings): 21" wide x 16" tall

Cut 2 Pockets: 5" wide x 5¾" tall

STEP 2. make the utensil pockets

On the utensil pocket pieces, with the **Wrong** side of the fabric facing up, on one 5" side, fold over ¼" toward the center of the pocket, then press. Fold over another ½" and press. Machine stitch a ⁵⁄₁₆" seam, making sure you stitch through all layers of fabric. This edge will become the top of the pocket. On the remaining three sides, with the **Wrong** side of the fabric facing up, fold over ¼" toward the center of the pocket, then press. Fold over another ¼" and press.

STEP 3. stitch the utensil pocket to the placemat

A. With the **Right** sides facing up, pin the utensil pocket to the front side of the placemat, aligning the utensil pocket on the **Right** side of the placemat, approximately 2" in from one shorter side edge and 3" up from the longer bottom edge. Make sure the finished, stitched edge of the pocket opens toward the top edge of the placemat. Stitch the pocket to the placemat, ⅛" from the outside edges of the pocket, down one long side, across the bottom, then up the other long side, backstitching at each end. Press.

B. Use a ruler and fadeout fabric marker to mark the stitching lines to make the pockets for each utensil. Mark a line 1¼" in from the left stitched edge of the pocket, and 1¼" in from the right stitched edge of the pocket. Make sure the lines are perpendicular to the top and bottom, and parallel to each other. To finish the slots, stitch on each marked line, beginning at the bottom and stitching toward the top edge of the pocket. Backstitch at each end.

STEP 4. make the placemat

A. Fold the ribbon in half. Pin the folded end of the ribbon to the left side of the front of the placemat (opposite the utensil pocket) approximately 6½" up from the bottom edge.

B. With the **Right** sides together, pin the front side of the placemat (with the utensil pocket) to the lining of the placemat. The ribbon should be sandwiched between the layers. Stitch around all 4 sides, making sure to catch the folded end of the ribbon in the seam, and leaving a 3" opening on one side, back-stitching at each end.

C. Trim the corners.

D. Turn the placemat **Right**-side out. Use a point turner to push out the corners. (See page 141 for an explanation of a point turner.)

STEP 5. finish the placemat

Press the edges flat, making sure to enclose the raw edges of the opening. Pin the opening closed. Topstitch around all the sides, ¼" in from the finished edges. (See page 141 for an explanation of topstitching.)

STEP 6. follow the instructions in steps 2 through 5 to make the other placemat

go

simple tote

LEVEL 2   You cannot have too many tote bags. Especially after you discover how easy they are to sew! Combining different fabrics and experimenting with various sizes will give you endless possibilities. A book bag, a knitting tote, a gym carryall, a catch-all for the car—it makes a marvelous customized gift for anyone. This is an easy project, suitable for any level of skill with the sewing machine. For an added challenge, get creative with appliqué and embroidery. Once you get the hang of the pattern, try different sizes.

FABRICS

⅝ yard medium-weight cotton or linen (for the top panel and handles)

½ yard of contrasting cotton or linen (for the bottom panel)

SUPPLIES

Yardstick

Fabric marker

Scissors

Straight pins

notes

Preshrink fabric by washing, drying, and pressing before you start.

All seams are ½" unless otherwise stated. A ½" seam allowance is included in all cutting measurements.

CONTINUED

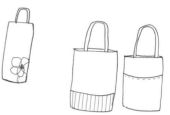

STEP 1. cut out all pieces from the fabric

Measure and mark the dimensions below directly onto the **Wrong** side of your fabric, using a yardstick and a fabric marker. Then, using your scissors cut out each piece, following the marked lines.

From the fabric for the top panel and handles of the tote:
Cut 1 Main Panel: 14" wide x 33" tall

Cut 2 Handles: 4" wide x 21" tall

From the contrasting fabric:
Cut 1 Bottom Panel: 14" wide x 11" tall

STEP 2. make the handles

A. With the **Wrong** side of one of the handle pieces facing up, on both 4" sides, fold over ½" toward the center of the handle and press. Trim the corners at a 45-degree angle to reduce the bulk, making sure not to clip the stitching. (See page 140 for an explanation of mitering corners.)

B. With the **Wrong** side of the handle piece facing up, fold each long side toward the center of the handle, so that the raw edges meet at the crease. Press, then fold it in half lengthwise. Press again. Edge stitch the three open sides of the handle by stitching close to the edge, beginning on one short side at the fold, then up the long side, and down the other short side. Make sure you stitch through all the layers of fabric. Backstitch at each end.

C. Repeat Steps 2A and 2B to make the other handle. Set both handles aside.

STEP 3. make the totebag

A. With the **Wrong** side of the bottom panel facing up, on each 14" side, fold over ½" toward the center of the panel, then press. This creates the top edge of the bottom panel. With the **Wrong** sides together, fold the bottom panel in half, matching up the opposite folded edges. Press a crease on the fold, then open the fabric with the **Right** side facing up. Set aside. *see figure 3A*

B. With the **Wrong** sides of the main panel together, fold it in half, matching up the two 14" sides. Press a crease on the fold, then open the fabric with the **Right** side facing up. With the **Right** side facing up, pin the bottom panel to the **Right** side of the main panel, matching up the creased center folds and the raw edges on the sides. *see figure 3B*

C. Being careful to keep center folds of both pieces aligned, edge stitch the two finished edges of the bottom panel to the main panel, making sure you stitch through all the layers of fabric.

D. With the **Right** sides together, fold the tote in half on the crease, matching up the raw edges. Pin in place, making sure the bottom panel has not shifted on the main panel. Stitch one side together, from the bottom folded edge to the top unfinished edge of the tote, backstitching at each end. Repeat for the other side of the tote. Press the seams open and stitch each raw edge with a zigzag stitch to keep the seams from fraying.

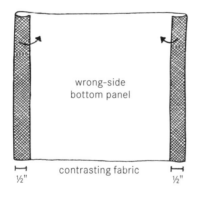

wrong-side
bottom panel

½" contrasting fabric ½"

FIGURE **3A**

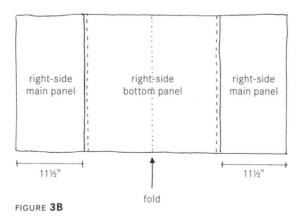

right-side
main panel

right-side
bottom panel

right-side
main panel

11½" 11½"

fold

FIGURE **3B**

CONTINUED

STEP 4. finish the tote

A. On the top (unstitched) edge, fold over ½" toward the **Wrong** side (inside of the tote), then press. Fold over another 1" and press. Stitch a ⅞" seam, making sure you stitch through all the layers. *see figure 4A*

B. To place the handles on one side of the tote, measure 4" in from each side seam. Mark the points with pins. Place the ends of the handles inside the tote, matching up the bottom edges of the handle with the finished hem of the tote 1" down from the top edge. Align the outside stitched edges of the handle with the pins, making sure the handle is not twisted.

C. Attach the handles by edge stitching a rectangle. With the **Wrong** side (inside) of the tote facing up, edge stitch the bottom edge of the handle to the tote, stopping just before you reach the side edge of the handle. Without lifting the needle out of the fabric, turn the tote 90 degrees and stitch down the next side, stopping just before you reach the top edge of the tote. Without lifting the needle, turn 90 degrees and stitch parallel to the top edge of the tote, stopping just before you reach the other side edge of the handle. Without lifting the needle, stitch down the other side edge of the handle to complete the rectangle. For added decoration, you can stitch an "X" inside the rectangles. *see figure 4C*

D. Repeat Steps 4B and 4C to attach the other handle to the opposite side of the tote.

E. Turn the bag **Right**-side out and press.

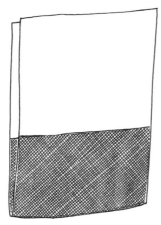

FIGURE **4A**

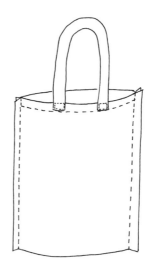

FIGURE **4C**

gardening tote

FINISHED SIZE: 16½" WIDE X 10½" TALL X 5" DEEP

LEVEL 4

This practical carryall is the perfect gardening tote. It is generously sized and will fit and organize your gardening tools, gloves, and all those bags of seeds. The middle compartment is roomy enough to hold your fresh flowers and vegetables as well. This project will require a few hours of your attention, and is suitable for the more experienced sewing machine user. To ensure a sturdy tote, pick a heavier fabric like canvas for the project.

FABRICS

2 yards heavy-weight cotton

1¾ yards (1" wide) twill tape

SUPPLIES

Scissors

Straight pins

Yardstick

Fadeout fabric marker

notes

Preshrink fabric by washing, drying, and pressing before you start.

All seams are ½" unless otherwise stated. A ½" seam allowance is included in all cutting measurements and pattern pieces.

CONTINUED

STEP 1. cut out all pieces from the fabric

A. Cut out the pattern pieces provided in the pocket on the inside cover of this book: Gardening Tote Front and Back Pockets, End Pocket, and Bottom.

B. Pin the pattern pieces to the fabric and, using your scissors, cut out each piece, following the solid cutting lines on the pattern pieces. Transfer the notch markings (for pleats) from the pattern to the fabric pieces by making ¼" clips into the seam allowances. Transfer the stitching lines for the front and back pockets using a fadeout fabric marker.

From the fabric:
Cut 2 Front and Back Pockets

Cut 2 End Pockets

Cut 2 Bottoms (1 will be the lining)

Additionally, you will need to measure, mark, and cut the following pieces from your fabric. To do so, measure and mark the dimensions below directly on to the **Wrong** side of your fabric using a yardstick and fadeout fabric marker. Then, using your scissors, cut out each piece, following the marked lines.

Cut 4 pieces for the End Panels (2 will be the lining): 6" wide x 11½" tall

Cut 4 pieces for the Front and Back Panels (2 will be the lining): 17½" wide x 11½" tall

Cut 2 pieces for the Handles: 4" wide x 17" long

C. With the **Right** sides of the front and back panels facing up, mark the stitching line placement of the pockets with a fadeout fabric marker 6½" in from the left side, and 6½" in from the right side.

STEP 2. make the pockets

A. Use a fadeout fabric marker to transfer the stitching lines from the pattern pieces onto the **Right** side of the front and back pockets.

B. Create two pleats in each of the two end pockets, by folding the fabric toward the center of the pocket, matching up the notches and pinning. Use the illustration as a guide. Each pleat will be ⅜" wide. Machine stitch the pleats in place, ¼" in from the raw edge. Set aside. *see figure 2B*

C. Create four pleats in both the front and back pockets, using the illustration as a guide. Each pleat will be ⅜" wide. Stitch the pleats in place, ¼" in from the raw edge. *see figure 2C*

D. With the **Right** sides together, pin the two pocket ends to the pocket front and pocket back, matching up the seams' raw edges. Stitch the pieces together, to create a tube of fabric.

CONTINUED

E. Fold the twill tape in half lengthwise and press. With the **Right** side of the pocket facing up, beginning on the left side of the pocket front, encase the top edge of the pockets with the folded twill tape, pinning as you go. You will have a "sandwich," with the top raw edge of the pockets placed flush with the center fold of the twill tape. Leave about 1" to overlap the starting end. Trim the excess twill tape. Fold the ending edge under ½" so that the raw edge is tucked in, and pin. Stitch the twill tape in place, using a ⅜" seam, making sure you stitch through all the layers. Set aside.

STEP 3. make the exterior and lining for the ends, front, and back of the tote

With the **Right** sides together, pin the two end panels to the front and back panels (for the exterior of the tote), matching up the seams' raw edges. Stitch the panels together, backstitching at each end, to create the tote's exterior fabric "tube." Repeat with the front, back, and the two end panels for the lining.

STEP 4. stitch the pockets to the exterior of the tote

With the **Wrong** side of the pocket tube facing the **Right** side of the exterior tube, match up the end seams and the stitching lines. Also, match up the lower raw edge of the pocket tube (pleated edge) with the lower end of the tote. Baste the pieces together, using a ¼" seam, and stitch the pocket tube to the exterior tube of the tote along the bottom edge. (See page 138 for an explanation of basting.)

STEP 5. stitch the bottom to the sides of the tote

A. Use a fadeout fabric marker to transfer the large dots and the clipping marks on the bottom pattern piece to the **Right** sides of the exterior bottom and the lining bottom. Use scissors to carefully clip no more than ¼" to ⅜" into the seam allowance.

B. With the **Right** sides together, pin the exterior bottom to the basted lower edge of the exterior tube, matching up the corners of the end panels with the large dots on the bottom. With the **Wrong** side of the bottom facing you, stitch around the bottom, backstitching at each end.

STEP 6. make the handles

With the **Wrong** side of one handle piece facing up, fold it in half lengthwise, then press a crease on the fold. Open the piece so that the **Wrong** side faces up. Fold the two long sides toward the crease, so that they meet at the crease. Press, then fold it in half lengthwise. Press again. Match up the long folded edges (opposite the crease), then stitch them together, using a ⅛" seam, backstitching at each end. Make sure you stitch through all the layers. Repeat this step to make the other handle. *see figure 6*

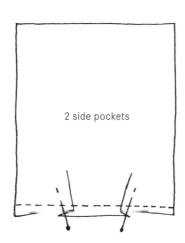

2 side pockets

FIGURE **2B**

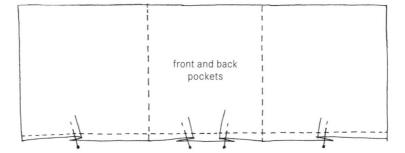

front and back
pockets

FIGURE **2C**

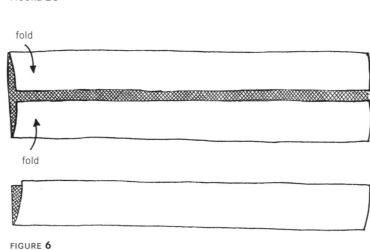

fold

fold

FIGURE **6**

CONTINUED

STEP 7. finish the tote

A. To mark the location of the handles, on the exterior front panel of the tote, measure 5" from each seam that joins the front panel to the end panels and place a pin.

B. With the **Right** sides together, pin one handle to the **Wrong** side of the exterior front panel, matching up the raw edges of the ends of the handle with the raw edge of the top of the tote. Baste the handle in place, using a ¼" seam. Repeat with the handle for the exterior back panel of the tote.

C. With the **Right** sides together, pin the exterior of the tote to the tote lining, matching up the raw edges and side seams. The handles will be sandwiched between the two layers. Stitch together around the tote, leaving a 4" opening and backstitching at each end.

D. Turn the tote **Right**-side out, tucking the lining into the tote and pulling out the handles. To enclose the raw edges at the opening, fold the raw edges under ½" and pin the opening closed. Press. Slip stitch the opening closed by hand. If you prefer, edge stitch the opening closed by machine. Press. (See page 141 for an explanation of slip stitching.)

E. Topstitch around the top edge of the tote, ¼" in from the finished edge. (See page 141 for an explanation of topstitching.)

yoga mat tote

FINISHED SIZE: 8" WIDE X 30" TALL WHEN FLAT

LEVEL 2 This tote is not only practical for transporting your yoga mat, it is a great way to combine function with style in your everyday life. And, if you're like me, you still need a pocket for your cell phone, even on your way to yoga class! This is a fun project, especially if you're experienced with a sewing machine.

FABRICS

¾ yard medium- to heavy-weight cotton or linen

¾ yard (approximately ¼" thick) cord to coordinate with your fabric.

SUPPLIES

Yardstick

Fabric marker

Scissors

Straight pins

notes

Preshrink fabric by washing, drying, and pressing before you start.

All seams are ½" unless otherwise stated. A ½" seam allowance is included in all cutting measurements.

CONTINUED

STEP 1. cut out all pieces from the fabric

Measure and mark the dimensions below directly onto the **Wrong** side of your fabric, using a yardstick and a fabric marker. Then, using your scissors, cut out each piece, following the marked lines.

Cut 1 piece for the body of the Bag: 17" wide x 32" tall

Cut 1 piece for the Strap: 5½" wide x 40" long

Cut 1 piece for the Outside Pocket: 6" wide x 13" long

STEP 2. make the pocket

With the **Right** sides together, fold the pocket in half widthwise so you have a piece that measures 6" x 6½". Stitch along each 6½" side. Turn **Right**-side out. Fold in the open edge 1½" and press. Pin the pocket on the bag piece 3" up from one 17" edge and 2" in from one 32" edge, making sure the folded-in edge is at the bottom. Stitch down one side, across the bottom and up the other side, backstitching at the beginning and end.

STEP 3. make the strap

A. Fold the strap in half lengthwise, matching raw edges, and stitch down the 39" edge using a ½" seam allowance, backstitching at each end.

B. Turn right-side out and press.

CONTINUED

STEP 4. assemble the bag

A. With the **Right** sides together, fold the bag in half lengthwise, matching up the raw edges. Center one end of the strap along the bottom edge of the bag, sandwiched between the two layers. Stitch across the bottom and up the side of the bag, stopping 2½" from the top and backstitching. Stitch again from the top down 1½", leaving a 1" opening. Press the side seam open. Fold the top edge down toward the **Wrong** side ½" and press, then fold another 1" and press. Stitch down close to the edge. Bring the strap up along the side without the pocket. Fold the edge under ½" and press. Pin the folded edge to the bag under the stitching line on the top edge. Stitch close to the top edge, down one side approximately ⅜", across to the other side and up ⅜", making a rectangle. *see figure 4A*

B. Knot each end of the cord so they don't unravel. Thread the cord through the casing.

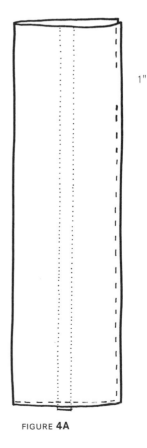

1"

FIGURE **4A**

all-day tote

FINISHED SIZE: 14" WIDE X 10" TALL X 6" DEEP

LEVEL 3

This bag has it all! There are plenty of pockets for all your different needs throughout the day: keys, phone, change, morning paper, and all the etceteras. Choose fabrics you adore, and you'll want to carry it all day, every day. The tote project will take a day or two to complete, even if you are experienced with your sewing machine. Pick a sturdy fabric such as canvas for this project.

FABRICS

1 yard medium- to heavy-weight cotton or linen for Bag

1 yard of medium-weight cotton for Lining

½ yard (1" wide) twill tape

SUPPLIES

Yardstick

Fadeout fabric marker (or tailor's chalk)

Scissors

Straight pins

Ruler

½" diameter metal key ring

One quick-release key clip

notes

Preshrink fabric by washing, drying, and pressing before you start.

All seams are ½" unless otherwise stated. A ½" seam allowance is included in all cutting measurements.

Metal key rings and plastic or metal quick-release key clips can be found at hardware and craft stores, or places where keys are made.

CONTINUED

STEP 1. cut out all pieces from the fabric

Measure and mark the dimensions below directly onto the **Wrong** side of your fabric, using a yardstick and a fadeout fabric marker. Then, using your scissors, cut out each piece following the marked lines.

From the fabric for the Exterior of the Tote
Cut 1 Bottom Panel: 7" wide x 15" long

Cut 2 Front and Back Panels: 15" wide x 11" tall

Cut 2 End Panels: 7" wide x 11" tall

Cut 1 End Panel Pocket: 7" wide x 7" tall

Cut 1 Front Panel Pocket: 10" wide x 11" tall

Cut 2 Handles: 4" wide X 15" long

From the fabric for the Lining of the Tote
Cut 1 Bottom Panel: 7" wide x 15" long

Cut 2 Front and Back Panels: 15" wide x 11" tall

Cut 2 Side Panels: 7" wide x 11" tall

Cut 1 Inside Side Panel Pocket: 7" wide x 5" tall

STEP 2. make the exterior end panel

A. With the **Wrong** side of the end panel pocket piece facing up, on one 7" side, fold over ¼" toward the center of the pocket, then press. Fold over another ¼" and press. Machine stitch a ³⁄₁₆" seam, making sure you stitch through all the layers of fabric. Set aside.

B. With the **Right** sides facing up, pin the pocket to one of the end panels, matching up the raw edges of the pocket with the two side edges and bottom edge of the end panel. Baste the pieces together using a ¼" seam. (See page 138 for an explanation of basting.)

STEP 3. make the front panel

A. From the twill tape, cut an 11" piece. Fold it in half lengthwise and press. With the **Right** side of the front panel pocket facing up, encase one 11" edge with the folded twill tape, pinning as you go. The raw edge of the pocket will be flush with the center fold of the twill tape. Stitch the twill tape in place, using a ³⁄₈" seam, making sure you stitch through all the layers.

B. With the **Right** sides facing up, pin the pocket to the front panel, matching up the bottom raw edges and raw edge of the left side of the pocket with the raw edge of the left side of the front panel. Baste in place using a ¼" seam. Along the twill-taped edge, stitch the pocket to the front panel, about 2" up from the bottom edge, backstitching at each end. *see figure 3B*

CONTINUED

STEP 4. finish the exterior of the tote

A. With the **Right** sides together, pin the end panel with the pocket to the left side of the front panel, matching up the raw edges of the bottom of the pocket with the raw edge of the bottom of the end panel. Stitch from the top edge to the bottom, stopping ½" from the bottom edge, backstitching at each end.

B. With the **Right** sides together, pin the other end panel to the right side of the front panel, matching up the top and bottom raw edges of both pieces. Stitch from the top edge to the bottom, stopping ½" from the bottom edge, backstitching at each end.

C. With the **Right** sides together, pin the two sides of the back panel to the end panels, matching up the raw edges. Stitch the panels together, from the top edge to the bottom, stopping ½" from the bottom edge, backstitching at each end. You have created the tote's exterior fabric tube.

D. With the **Right** sides together, pin the fabric tube to the bottom panel, matching up the tube's side seams with the corners of the bottom panel. The unstitched ½" of each side seam will split to each side of the bottom. Stitch around all four sides, backstitching at each end.

STEP 5. make the lining

A. Make the pocket for the lining back panel. With the **Wrong** side of the pocket facing up, on one 7" side, fold over ¼" toward the center of the pocket, then press. Fold over another ¼" and press. Stitch a ³⁄₁₆" seam, making sure you stitch through all the layers.

B. On the remaining three sides, with the **Wrong** side facing up, fold over ¼" toward the center of the pocket, then press. Fold over another ¼" and press.

C. With the **Right** sides facing up, pin the pocket to the lining back panel, referring to the illustration. Edge stitch the pocket in place, down one side, across the bottom, then up the other side. *see figure 5C*

D. Use a ruler and fadeout fabric marker to mark the stitching line on the pocket, 2" from the right edge. Make sure the line is perpendicular to the top and bottom, and parallel to the side edge of the pocket.

E. Follow steps 4A through 4D to complete the lining.

STEP 6. make the handles

With the **Wrong** side of a handle piece facing up, fold it in half lengthwise, then press a crease on the fold. Open the piece so that the **Wrong** side faces up. Fold the two long sides toward the crease, matching up the raw edges at the crease. Press, then fold it in half lengthwise. Press again. Match up the long folded edges (opposite the crease), then edge stitch them together, backstitching at each end. Make sure you stitch through all layers of fabric. Repeat this step to make the other handle.

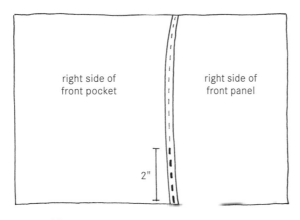

right side of
front pocket

right side of
front panel

2"

FIGURE **3B**

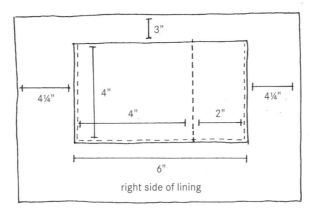

3"

4¼"

4"

4"

2"

4¼"

6"

right side of lining

FIGURE **5C**

CONTINUED

STEP 7. make the key strap

Take a 6" piece of twill tape, fold under ½" of one of the short ends and press. Then fold the twill tape in half lengthwise and press. Fold the finished edge of the twill tape through the key ring. Stitch the tape in place. Next, edge stitch the long, unfolded edge of the twill tape, backstitching each end.

STEP 8. finish the tote

A. To mark the location of the handles, on the **Right** side of the lining front panel of the tote, measure 3" from each seam that joins the front panel to the end panels and mark with pins.

B. With the **Right** sides together, pin one handle to the lining front panel, matching up the raw edges of the ends of the handle with the raw edge of the top of the tote. Make sure the handle is not twisted. Baste the handle in place, using a ¼" seam. Repeat with the handle for the lining back panel of the tote.

C. Pin the key strap to the top edge of the **Right** side of the lining end panel.

D. With the **Right** sides together, pin the exterior of the tote to the tote lining, matching raw edges and side seams. The handles and key strap will be sandwiched between the two layers. Stitch the lining and exterior together, leaving a 4" opening on one side, and backstitching at each end. *see figure 8D*

E. Turn the tote right-side out, tucking the lining into the tote and pulling out the handles. To enclose the raw edges at the opening, fold the raw edges under ½" and pin the opening closed. Press. Slip stitch the opening closed by hand. If you prefer edge stitch the opening closed by machine. Press. (See page 141 for an explanation of slip stitching.)

F. Topstitch around the top edge of the tote, ¼" in from the finished edge. (See page 141 for an explanation of topstitching.)

G. Attach the quick-release key clip to the key strap.

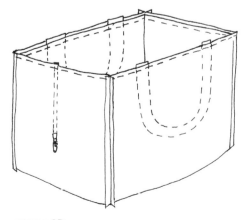

FIGURE **8D**

sun hat

FINISHED SIZE: ADULT MEDIUM

LEVEL 3 This timeless wide-brimmed sun hat is very stylish indeed, protecting you at the beach on your vacation or matched to your garden tote for those sunny days a little closer to home. Do something good for your skin and your soul by stitching this summery project. Making the sun hat requires some experience with sewing. Put aside a couple of evenings for this project.

FABRICS

¾ yard (44" wide) light- to medium-weight cotton for the hat

¾ yard (44" wide) light-weight cotton for the lining

¾ yard of fusible interfacing

SUPPLIES

Scissors

Straight pins

Hand sewing needle and thread

notes

Preshrink fabric by washing, drying, and pressing before you start.

All seams are ½" unless otherwise stated. A ½" seam allowance is included in all cutting measurements and is marked on the pattern pieces.

CONTINUED

STEP 1. cut out all pattern pieces from the fabric

A. Cut out all the hat pattern pieces provided in the pocket on the inside cover of this book: Hat Top, Crown, and Brim.

B. With the **Right** sides together, fold the hat fabric in half, matching up the raw edges. Pin the pattern pieces to the fabric, making sure you align the grain line marked on the pattern with the grain of the fabric. Using your scissors, cut out each piece, following the solid cutting lines on the pattern pieces. Repeat with the lining fabric. (See page 139 for an explanation of grain line and aligning pattern pieces on the grain of the fabric.) *see figure 1A+B*

C. Cut out the brim lining from the interfacing.

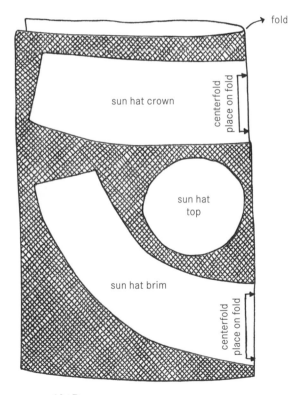

FIGURE **1A+B**

CONTINUED

STEP 2. make the hat

A. Fuse the interfacing to the lining brim following the manufacturer's instructions.

B. With the **Right** sides together, match up the raw edges of the center back of the hat brim. Pin in place, then machine stitch. Press the seam open. Repeat with the lining brim piece.

C. With the **Right** sides together, stitch the hat brim and lining brim together along the outside edge. Turn **Right**-side out and press. *see figure 2C*

D. Topstitch around the edge of the brim, ¼" in from the finished outside edge, backstitching when you return to the starting point. Stitch another row of topstitching, ¼" in from the last row of stitching. Continue in this manner until you are ½" from inside edge of the brim (where the brim joins the crown). (See page 141 for an explanation of topstitching.)

E. With the **Right** sides together, match up the raw edges of the center back of the crown. Pin, then stitch together. Press the seam open. *see figure 2E*

F. With the **Right** sides together, pin the brim to the crown, clipping the curved seam allowance so that it lays flat. Make sure you do not clip more than ⅜" into the seam allowance. Stitch together.

G. With the **Right** sides together, pin the top to the crown, clipping the crown along the curved seam so that it lays flat. Make sure you do not clip more than ⅜" into the seam allowance. Stitch together. *see figure 2G*

H. Repeat Steps 2D through F to make the lining.

I. With the **Wrong** side of the lining facing up, on the bottom edge of the crown, fold over ½" toward the top edge of the crown. Press.

STEP 3. finish the hat

A. Insert the lining into the hat, **Wrong**-sides together. Match up the center back seams of the lining with the hat. Pin the folded bottom edge of the crown lining to the crown of the hat, covering up the seam that joins the brim with the crown.

B. With the hand sewing needle and thread, slip stitch the folded edge of the crown lining to the inside edge of the brim. *see figure 3B*

FIGURE **2C**

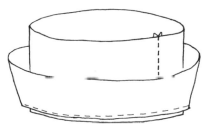

FIGURE **2E**

FIGURE **2G**

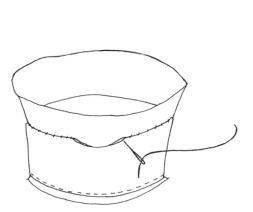

FIGURE **3B**

simple drawstring backpack

LEVEL 2

This basic design provides a practical and perfect-sized daypack. It is excellent to use for a packed lunch and a notebook on a stroll in the hills, or maybe for holding your essentials when you're walking through the farmers' market. The construction of the backpack is fairly simple, but allow a day for this project. It is a good project for a beginner who is ready for a little challenge.

FABRICS

1½ yards (44" wide) medium-weight cotton or linen

SUPPLIES

Yardstick

Fadeout fabric marker (or tailor's chalk)

Scissors

Straight pins

Ruler

Large safety pin

notes

Preshrink fabric by washing, drying, and pressing before you start.

All seams are ½" unless otherwise stated. A ½" seam allowance is included in all cutting measurements.

CONTINUED

STEP 1. cut out all pieces from the fabric

Measure and mark the dimensions below directly onto the **Wrong** side of your fabric, using a yardstick and a fadeout fabric marker. Then, using your scissors, cut out each piece following the marked lines.

From the fabric:

Cut 1 Bag: 13" wide x 33½" long

Cut 1 Pocket: 13" wide x 9½" long

Cut 2 Straps: 4" wide x 54" long

STEP 2. make the straps

With the **Wrong** side facing up, fold each long edge inward to meet in the center and press. Fold the handle in half lengthwise and press again. Stitch along the long open edge. Repeat this step to make the other strap. Set them aside.

STEP 3. make the backpack pockets and bag

A. Hem the top edge of the pocket. With the **Wrong** side of the pocket piece facing up, fold one 13" edge over ¼" and press. Then fold over ½" and press. Machine stitch a ⅜" seam, making sure you stitch through all the layers.

B. Stitch the hemmed pocket piece to the front of the bag: With the **Right** side of the bag piece facing up, fold the piece in half, matching up the raw edges of the 13" top and bottom sides. Press. Open bag again and, using a fadeout fabric marker and yardstick, draw a parallel line 1" to the right of the fold. With the **Right** sides together, match up the raw (unhemmed) edge of the pocket piece with the drawn line. The hemmed edge of the pocket will lie on top of the back of the bag piece as shown in the illustration. Pin in place. Stitch the pocket piece to the bag piece, using a ½" seam in from the raw edge of the pocket piece. *see figure 3B*

C. Finish the pockets. Flip the pocket back so that the **Right** side is facing up and press. To create separate pockets, use a fadeout fabric marker and ruler to mark a line 7½" in from each raw edge to create two equal-sized pockets (if you want to make different-sized pockets to fit your own needs, make your lines accordingly). Stitch on top of the lines, backstitching at each end. Press.

D. Fold the bag piece in half widthwise so the 13" sides meet, **Right**-sides together, matching up the side and top edges. Pin the side edges in place, making sure the raw edges of the pocket piece are matched up with the raw edges of the sides. Beginning 3" down from the top edge, and stopping 2" before you reach the bottom folded edge, stitch the sides together using a ½" seam.

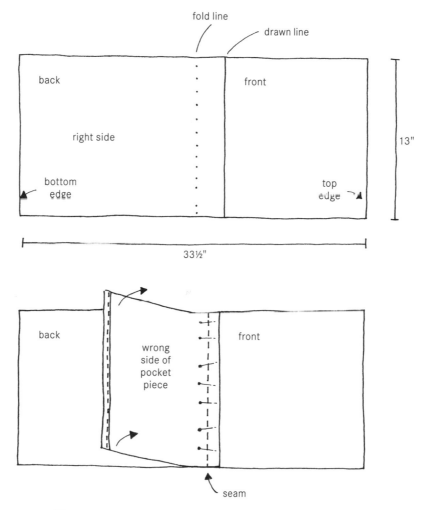

FIGURE **3B**

CONTINUED

E. Create a casing for the straps. With the **Wrong** side of the bag facing up, press the seam allowance open at one of the top edges. Fold the top edge over ¼", then press. Fold over 1¼" and press. Stitch a 1⅛" seam, making sure you stitch through all the layers. Repeat this step on the other top edge of the bag. Turn the bag **Right**-side out.

STEP 4. thread the straps through the casings

A. With the **Right** side facing out, lay the backpack flat with the strap casings parallel to one another in front of you as shown. Take the first strap and, with the long hemmed edge of the strap facing the bottom of the bag, thread it through the top casing from right to left, then through the bottom casing from left to right. Attaching a large safety pin to the strap will help you thread it through the hole. Being careful that the strap is not twisted, pin the two ends of the strap together. *see figure 4A+B, view 1*

B. Take the second strap and, again orienting the long hemmed edge with the bottom of the casing, thread it through the casings in the opposite direction. That is, through the top casing from left to right and the bottom casing from right to left. Being sure that the strap has not become twisted, pin the two ends together. The straps will form two U shapes, facing opposite directions. *see figure 4A+B, view 2*

STEP 5. finish the drawstring backpack

A. With the backpack laying flat, take the pinned ends of the strap on the right-hand side and tuck them into the opening at the right bottom corner of the bag. Then tuck the strap ends on the left side into the opening at the left bottom corner of the bag.

B. Turn the backpack **Wrong**-side out, making sure the straps do not twist. Remove the pin that is holding the two ends of the first strap together. Match up the raw short ends with the side seams. Pin in place. Stitch the opening closed, backstitching at each end.

Repeat with the strap ends on the opposite side. Turn the backpack **Right**-side out. Press.

view 1 from above

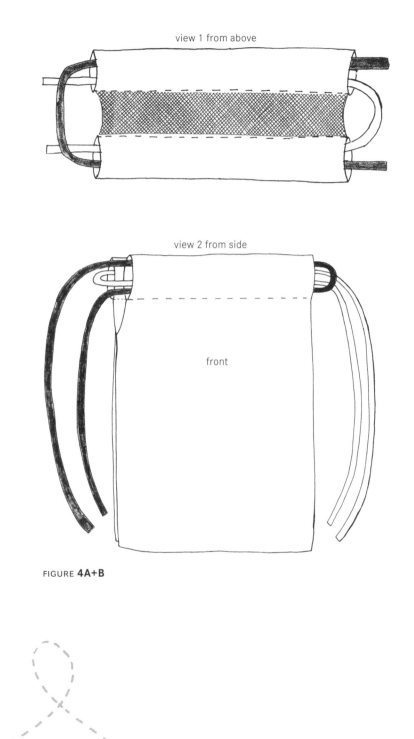

view 2 from side

front

FIGURE **4A+B**

nest

curtain with pockets

LEVEL 2 A curtain, a room divider, even a wall hanging, this project will add a creative touch to your home while providing a separation between two spaces—whether it's outside or between a work space and sleeping area. The pockets might hold test tubes for flowers or a small, budding branch in spring, bringing the natural world into even the most urban setting. This design has three pockets, but feel free to add more or change their size for your own trinkets and treasures.

FABRICS

Light- to medium-weight cotton or linen (Your yardage will vary. See worksheet.)

SUPPLIES

½" curtain rod; the width depends on the desired width of your curtain

Yardstick

Fabric marker

Scissors

Straight pins

3 to 6 glass test tubes, size: 6" tall x 1¼" around (150mm x 25mm)*

See resource guide for suggestions of where to buy test tubes.

notes

The width and length will depend on the measurements of the area you want to cover. Use the following worksheet to determine the amount of fabric required.

Preshrink fabric by washing, drying, and pressing before you start.

All seams are ½" unless otherwise stated. A ½" seam allowance is included in all cutting measurements.

MEASUREMENT WORKSHEET

Number of Panels

1. Measure the width of the rod: _____

2. Add 4½" (for two 2" side hems with ¼" turn under): _____

3. Divide by the usable fabric width: 42" or 54": _____

4. Round up to the nearest whole number for the number of full-width panels: _____

Length

1. Measure from the top edge of the rod to the desired length: _____

2. Add 4¼" for top hem and rod pocket: _____

3. Add 4¼" for bottom hem: _____

4. Add 12" for the Test Tube Pockets: _____

To calculate the total yardage required, multiply the length of each panel by the total number of panels above.

CONTINUED

STEP 1. mount the curtain rod

Install the rod over the window (or other desired space), before you take your measurements.

STEP 2. measure the window

Use the worksheet to record the measurements, determine the number of panels to cut, and the panel lengths. A panel can be cut lengthwise and joined with each side of the center panel, if additional width is needed.

STEP 3. cut out all pieces from the fabric

Measure and mark your dimensions directly onto the **Wrong** side of your fabric, using a yardstick and a fabric marker. Then, using your scissors, cut out each piece, following the marked lines.

Cut 4 Pockets: 4" wide x 12" long

STEP 4. make the curtain

A. If the width of your curtain requires more than one panel, with the **Right** sides together, match up the raw edges on the sides of the panels. Stitch the panels together and press.

B. With the **Wrong** side of the curtain panel facing up, on the left and right sides of the panel, fold over ¼" toward the center of the panel and press. Then fold another 2" and press. Machine stitch a seam ³⁄₁₆" from the folded edges to finish the two side hems.

C. With the **Wrong** side of the curtain panel facing up, on the top edge of the panel, fold over ¼" toward the center of the panel and press. Then fold over 2" and press. Machine stitch a seam ³⁄₁₆" from the folded edge to finish the top rod pocket.

D. With the **Wrong** side facing up, on the bottom edge of the panel, fold over ¼" toward the center of the panel and press. Then fold another 2" and press. Machine stitch a seam ³⁄₁₆" from the folded edge to finish the bottom hem.

STEP 5. make the test-tube pockets

With the **Right** sides together, fold one pocket piece in half widthwise. Stitch ¼" seam on each long side edge. Trim the corners at a 45-degree angle to reduce the bulk, making sure not to clip the stitching. Turn the pocket **Right**-side out and press. Fold the bottom raw edge up ½" toward the inside of the pocket and press. Repeat this step to make the other two pockets. (See page 140 for an explanation of mitering corners.)

STEP 6. finish the curtain

Slide the curtain onto the curtain rod. At about eye level, measure 3" in from the left edge of the curtain and pin the left edge of the first pocket in place, referring to the illustration below. Make sure the folded top edge of the pocket is oriented toward the top of the curtain. Again referring to the illustration below, pin the other two pockets in place. Make sure they are all parallel to each other. Edge stitch each pocket in place, down one side, across the bottom, then up the other side, backstitching at both ends. *see figure 6*

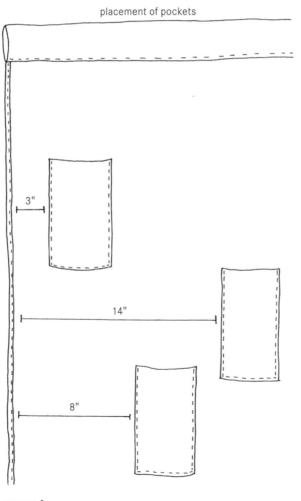

placement of pockets

FIGURE **6**

duvet cover

LEVEL 2

Here is another way to surround yourself with patterns, prints, and colors you love, both day and night. Make a matching set with pillowcases, or mix patterns and colors for a truly unique look. This project might seem overwhelming because of the amount of fabric you need to maneuver, but it is actually quite simple to sew. It is suitable for anyone familiar with a sewing machine.

FABRICS

Twin: 8 yards light-weight cotton

Queen: 10 yards light-weight cotton

King: 12 yards light-weight cotton

SUPPLIES

Yardstick

Fabric marker

Scissors

Straight pins

notes

Preshrink fabric by washing, drying, and pressing before you start.

All seams are ½" unless otherwise stated. A ½" seam allowance is included in all cutting measurements.

CONTINUED

STEP 1. cut out all pieces from the fabric

Measure and mark the dimensions below directly onto the **Wrong** side of your fabric, using a yardstick and a fabric marker. Then, using your scissors, cut out each piece, following the marked lines.

For a twin-size bed:
Cut 3 Wide Panels: 45" wide x 69" long

Cut 2 Narrow Panels: 25½" wide x 69" long

Cut 12 Ties: 2" wide x 9" long

For a queen-size bed:
Cut 3 Wide Panels: 45" wide x 89" long

Cut 2 Narrow Panels: 25½" wide x 89" long

Cut 16 Ties: 2" wide x 9" long

For a king-size bed:
Cut 3 Wide Panels: 45" wide x 105" long

Cut 2 Narrow Panels: 25½" wide x 105" long

Cut 18 Ties: 2" wide x 9" long

STEP 2. sew the panels together

Sew the panels together in this order: one narrow panel, three wide panels, and last, the second narrow panel. Match the long sides of two panels **Right**-sides together, then pin and seam. Continue in this manner until all five panels are sewn together. Press the seams to one side, and, using the zigzag stitch on your machine, zigzag the edges to prevent fraying. You should now have a piece that measures 182" x 69" for a twin, 182" x 89" for a queen, or 182" x 105" for a king. *see figure 2*

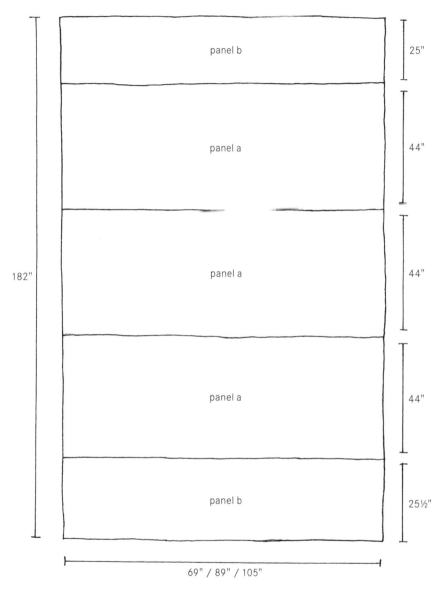

panel b — 25"

panel a — 44"

panel a — 44"

panel a — 44"

panel b — 25½"

182"

69" / 89" / 105"

FIGURE **2**

CONTINUED

STEP 3. sew the duvet cover

A. Fold the duvet cover in half, **Right**-sides together, matching up the raw edges of the two narrow panels and the panel seams along the sides. Stitch down each side, from the folded edge to the open end, as shown, backstitching at the beginning and end. Press the seams to one side, and using the zigzag stitch on your machine, zigzag the edges to prevent fraying. *see figure 3A*

B. On the open bottom edge, fold over ½" toward the **Wrong** side and press, then fold over another 1" and press. Topstitch around the bottom using a ⅞" seam allowance, making sure to backstitch at the beginning and the end.

STEP 4. add the ties

A. Make the ties as follows: Fold under ½" of each short end toward the **Wrong** side and press. Trim diagonally at the folded corners. Fold in each long edge to meet in the center and press. Then fold the strap in half lengthwise and press again. Making sure to backstitch at the beginning and the end, stitch down one short end, leaving the needle in the fabric, turn 90 degrees and stitch along the long open edge, again leave the needle in the fabric, turn 90 degrees and stitch up the other short folded under end. Do the same for the other ties.

B. Attach the ties. Take half the ties and space them evenly over the top half of the duvet cover opening. For each tie, pin 1" of one short end to the **Wrong** side (the inside) of the duvet cover. Attach the ties by stitching back and forth a few times at the edge of the tie and again near the edge of the duvet cover. Take the remaining ties and pin them to the bottom half of the duvet cover opening, being careful to line them up with the ties already in place. Sew these ties in place in the same way. *see figure 4B*

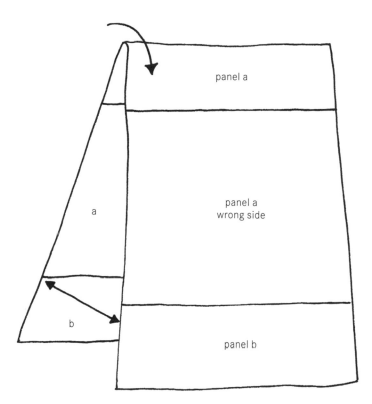

panel a

panel a
wrong side

a

b

panel b

FIGURE **3A**

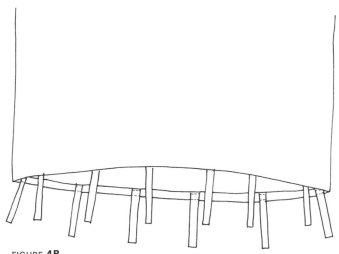

FIGURE **4B**

pillowcase

LEVEL 1

There is a certain satisfaction in resting your head on your own homemade pillowcase. When you discover how easy they really are to make you can whip them out by the dozens! This project is very easy, and suitable for beginners at sewing. The instructions below will help you customize the size to fit your pillow. This is a perfect project to enhance with some embroidery designs, or perhaps a monogram, for a custom touch.

FABRICS *(for a set of 2)*
1⅞ yards (44" wide) light-weight cotton

SUPPLIES
Yardstick

Fabric marker

Scissors

Straight pins

Point turner

notes
Preshrink fabric by washing, drying, and pressing before you start.

All seams are ½" unless otherwise stated. A ½" seam allowance is included in all cutting measurements.

CONTINUED

STEP 1. cut out all pieces from the fabric

Measure and mark the dimensions below directly onto the **Wrong** side of your fabric, using a yardstick and a fabric marker. Then, using your scissors, cut out each piece, following the marked lines.

For standard-size pillows:
Cut 2 pieces: 27" wide x 20" tall

Cut 2 pieces: 31" wide x 20" tall

For queen-size pillows:
Cut 2 pieces: 31" wide x 20" tall

Cut 2 pieces: 35" wide x 20" tall

For king-size pillows:
Cut 2 pieces: 37" wide x 20" tall

Cut 2 pieces: 41" wide x 20" tall

STEP 2. make the pillowcases

A. Lay one of the smaller pieces **Wrong**-side up. On one of the 20" sides, fold over ¼" and press, fold over another ¼" and press. Machine stitch using a ³⁄₁₆" seam allowance.

B. Lay one of the larger pieces **Wrong**-side up. On one of the 20" sides, fold over ¼" and press, fold over another ¼" and press. Stitch using a ³⁄₁₆" seam allowance. Fold over 4" and press; this will create the closing pocket.

C. With **Right**-sides together, pin the remaining 3 raw edges together. Take the 4" flap and fold it over the opening to the opposite side and pin, matching the raw edges of the pillowcase. You will have completely enclosed the pillowcase opening, which seems wrong, but don't worry, it will come out right. *see figure 2C*

D. Stitch using a ½" seam allowance, making sure to catch the flap piece in the seam. *see figure 2D*

E. Using your scissors, trim the corners at a 45-degree angle to reduce the bulk. Make sure you do not clip into your stitching.

F. Using the zigzag stitch on your sewing machine, stitch around the three raw edges to prevent them from fraying.

G. Turn the flap over to the other side, then turn the pillowcase **Right**-side out, using a point turner to push out the corners. (See page 141 for an explanation of a point turner.)

STEP 3. repeat steps A–G to make the other pillowcase

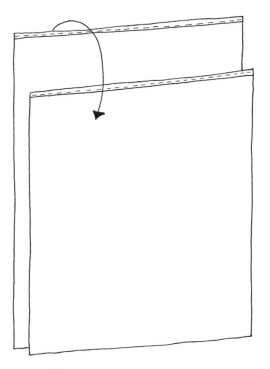

FIGURE **2C**

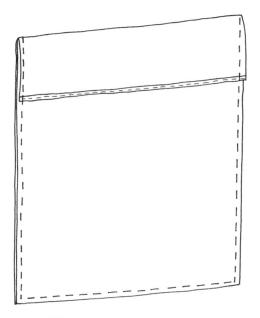

FIGURE **2D**

draft snake

FINISHED SIZE: 3" WIDE X 36" LONG

LEVEL 2   This project is an easy way to use up small scraps of fabric to make something very useful for your home. Place draft snakes in window sashes or at the base of a door to keep your house warm and toasty. This project is perfect for beginners as well as more experienced users of sewing equipment.

FABRICS
Small pieces of coordinating medium-weight fabric pieces (enough to complete a patchwork piece measuring 4" wide x 36" long)

SUPPLIES
Ruler

Fabric marker

Scissors

Straight pins

Hand sewing needle and thread

Point turner

5 lb. bag of rice or dried beans

notes
Preshrink fabric by washing, drying, and pressing before you start.

All seams are ½" unless otherwise stated. A ½" seam allowance is included in all cutting measurements.

CONTINUED

STEP 1. cut all pieces for the patchwork

You will find it helpful to lay your fabric pieces before beginning to stitch, so that you can see what the finished piece will look like and arrange the pieces to achieve the most pleasing pattern. *see figure 1*

The illustration shows the dimension of each patchwork piece used to make our sample. This is meant only as a guide. You may wish to follow our layout or create your own.

Cut 1 piece: 7" wide x 7" tall

Cut 1 piece: 19" wide x 7" tall

Cut 1 piece: 13" wide x 7" tall

If you wish to make a snake with more (or fewer) pieces, just remember that the combined widths of the pieces should equal 36" plus a 1" seam allowance per piece.

STEP 2. make the patchwork piece

A. Measure and mark the dimensions you want onto the **Wrong** side of your fabrics, using a ruler and fabric marker. Then, using your scissors, cut out each piece, following the marked lines.

B. Arrange the patchwork pieces as desired. With the **Right** sides together, seam the 7" sides of the pieces together, creating a strip 37" wide x 7" tall. Press each seam open. *see figure 2B*

STEP 3. make the draft snake

A. Fold the patchwork piece in half lengthwise, **Right**-sides together. Machine stitch a ½" seam along the length of the snake, stopping ½" from the bottom, turn the snake 90 degrees without lifting the needle out of the fabric, and stitch the short end, using a ½" seam. Backstitch at each end. *see figure 3A*

B. Turn the snake **Right**-side out. Push out the corners with a point turner. Fill with dried beans or rice. Turn the raw edges of the opening ½" inside the snake and pin in place. With the hand sewing needle and thread, slip stitch the opening closed. If you prefer, you can machine stitch close to the edge. (See page 141 for explanations of a point turner and slip stitching.)

FIGURE **1**

FIGURE **2B**

FIGURE **3A**

doorstop

FINISHED SIZE: 7" WIDE X 8" HIGH

LEVEL 4

The doorstop is an unusual and functional way to display your special fabrics at home. It is filled with dry beans or rice for weight. The practical handle makes it easy to move the doorstop around. This project will only take a couple of hours to complete if you are familiar with your sewing machine.

FABRICS

½ yard (44" wide) of medium- to heavy-weight cotton

SUPPLIES

Scissors

Straight pins

Ruler

Fabric marker

5 lb. bag of dried beans

Point turner

Hand sewing needle and thread

notes

Preshrink fabric by washing, drying, and pressing before you start.

All seams are ½" unless otherwise stated. A ½" seam allowance is included in all cutting measurements and is marked on the pattern pieces.

STEP 1. cut out all pattern pieces from the fabric

A. Cut out all Doorstop pieces provided in the pocket on the inside cover of this book: Doorstop Top, Bottom, and Side.

B. Pin the pattern pieces to the fabric, making sure you align the grain line marked on the pattern with the grain of the fabric. Using your scissors, cut out each piece, following the solid cutting lines on the pattern pieces. (See page 139 for an explanation of grain line and aligning pattern pieces with the grain of the fabric.)

From the fabric:

Cut 1 Top

Cut 4 Sides

Cut 1 Bottom

C. Additionally, measure and mark the dimensions below for the handle onto the **Wrong** side of your fabric, using a ruler and a fabric marker. Then, using your scissors, cut out the handle piece following the marked lines.

Cut 1 Handle: 4" wide x 8" long

CONTINUED

STEP 2. make the handle

A. With the **Wrong** side of the handle fabric facing up, on both 4" sides, fold over ½" toward the center of the handle and press. Trim the corners at a 45-degree angle to reduce the bulk.

B. With the **Wrong** side of handle fabric facing up, on both long sides, fold over 1" toward the center of the handle, then press. Next, fold the handle in half lengthwise and press again. Stitch up one short end, along the long open edge, and down the other end. *see figure 2A+B*

STEP 3. make the top

A. Pin the handle to the top, approximately ¾" in from two opposite side edges, and centered 3¼" from the other two opposite edges.

B. Attach the handle to the top by stitching a rectangle. Follow these steps: Stitching close to the edge, sew one short end of the handle onto the top, then without lifting the needle from the fabric turn 90 degrees and stitch toward the center of the handle about ½". Stop, then without lifting the needle from the fabric, turn 90 degrees and stitch parallel to the first line. Stop, and without lifting the needle from the fabric, turn 90 degrees and stitch toward the beginning point. You have completed a stitched rectangle. Repeat this step to attach the other end of the handle to the top. For added decoration, you can stitch an X inside the rectangles. Set aside. *see figure 3B*

STEP 4. attach the top to the sides

A. With the **Right** sides together, place two side pieces together, matching up the raw edges. Starting ½" from the end, stitch a ½" seam along the matched raw edges, stopping ½" from the end. Backstitch at each end. Press the seam allowance open. Using this method, stitch the other three side pieces together. Finally, stitch the first side piece to the fourth side piece to make a tube. Use a ½" seam allowance, and start and end ½" from the top and bottom edges.

B. With the **Right** sides together, and matching up the raw edges, pin the tube that you completed in Step 2A to the top. Make sure you match the corners of the top with the corners of the tube. Using a ½" seam, stitch them together, backstitching at each end. Also, make sure you stitch through both layers, especially when turning corners. Press toward the sides.

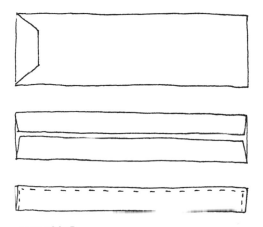

FIGURE **2A+B**

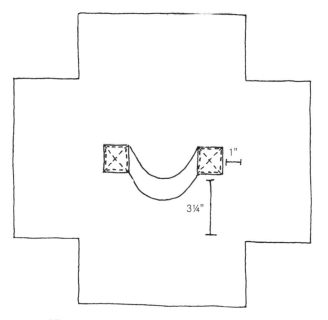

3¼"

1"

FIGURE **3B**

CONTINUED

STEP 5. attach the sides and top to the bottom

With the **Right** sides together, pin the sides to the bottom. Make sure you match the corners of the bottom with the corners of the sides. Using a ½" seam, stitch around all 4 sides, leaving a 4" opening on one side, and back-stitching at each end. Make sure you stitch through both layers, especially when turning and stitching corners. Press toward the bottom. *see figure 5*

STEP 6. finish the doorstop

Turn the doorstop **Right**-side out. Use a point turner to push out all of the corners. At the 4" opening, fold both edges under ½" and press. Fill the door-stop with beans. Then, with the hand sewing needle and thread, slip stitch the opening closed. If you prefer, you can machine stitch close to the edge. (See page 141 for explanations of a point turner and slip stitching.)

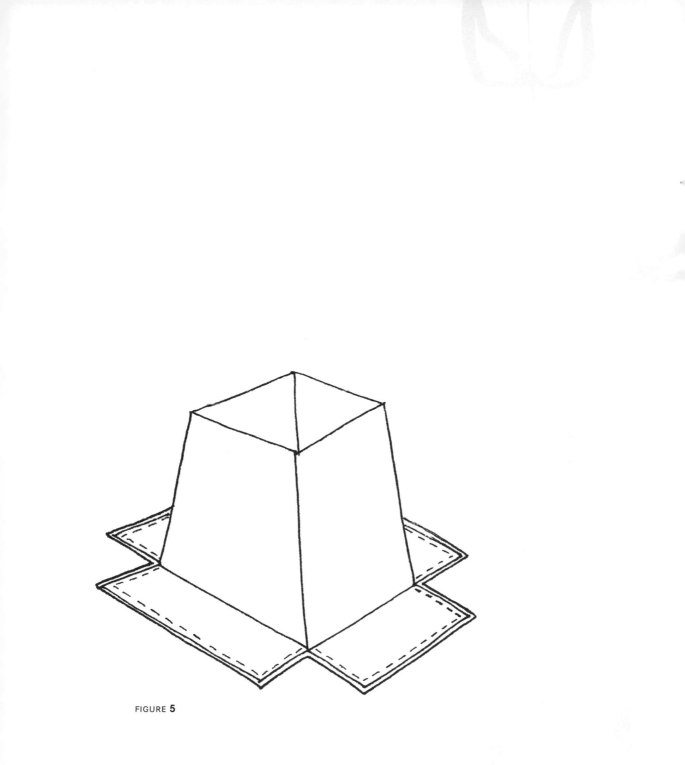

FIGURE **5**

organize

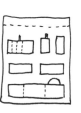

wall organizer

LEVEL 2

This is a pretty alternative to messy drawers. It's perfect for your home office, nursery, or craft projects. This project is rather easy to take on, but requires some time. Use a sturdy fabric such as canvas so the pockets stand up properly. For this wall hanging we used fabrics in big bold patterns. You can mix and match different fabrics for the different pockets, or make all the pockets match . . . it's up to you!

FABRICS
1⅜ yards (44" wide) medium- to heavy-weight cotton

SUPPLIES
Yardstick

Fabric marker

Scissors

Ruler

Fadeout fabric marker (or tailor's chalk)

Straight pins

Point turner

notes
Preshrink fabric by washing, drying, and pressing before you start.

All seams are ½" unless otherwise stated. A ½" seam allowance is included in all cutting measurements.

CONTINUED

STEP 1. cut out all pieces from the fabric

Measure and mark the dimensions below directly onto the **Wrong** side of your fabric, using a yardstick and a fabric marker. Then, using your scissors, cut out each piece, following the marked lines.

Cut 2 pieces for Main Panel and Lining: 21" wide x 31" tall

Cut 1 Pocket A: 18½" wide x 7¼" tall

Cut 1 Pocket B: 10" wide x 5¼" tall

Cut 1 Pocket C: 10" wide x 5¼" tall

Cut 1 Pocket D: 7" wide x 6¼" tall

Cut 1 Pocket E: 4" wide x 6½" tall

Cut 1 Pocket F: 3½" wide x 7¼" tall

Cut 1 Rod Casing: 21" wide x 6" tall

STEP 2. make the pockets

A. Begin with pocket A. With the **Wrong** side of the fabric facing up, fold one 18½" edge over ¼" toward the center of the pocket, then press. Fold over another ½" and press. Machine stitch a 5/16" hem, making sure you stitch through all layers of fabric. On the remaining three sides, with the **Wrong** side of the fabric facing up, fold over ¼" toward the center of the pocket, then press. Fold over another ¼" and press. Set aside.

B. For pockets B and C. With the **Wrong** side of the fabric for pocket B facing up, fold one 10" edge over ¼" toward the center of the pocket, then press. Fold over another ½" and press. Machine stitch a 5/16" hem, making sure you stitch through all the layers. On the remaining three sides, with the **Wrong** side of the fabric facing up, fold over ¼" toward the center of the pocket, then press. Fold over another ¼" and press. Repeat for pocket C. Set aside.

C. For pocket D. With the **Wrong** side of fabric facing up, fold one 7" edge over ¼" toward the center of the pocket, then press. Fold over another ½" and press. Machine stitch a 5/16" hem, making sure you stitch through all the layers. On the remaining three sides, with the **Wrong** side of the fabric facing up, fold over ¼" toward the center of the pocket, then press. Fold over another ¼" and press. Set aside.

D. For pocket E. With the **Wrong** side of fabric facing up, fold one 4" edge over ¼" toward the center of the pocket, then press. Fold over another ½" and press. Machine stitch a 5/16" hem, making sure you stitch through all the layers. On the remaining three sides, with the **Wrong** side of the fabric facing up, fold over ¼" toward the center of the pocket, then press. Fold over another ¼" and press. Set aside.

placement of pockets

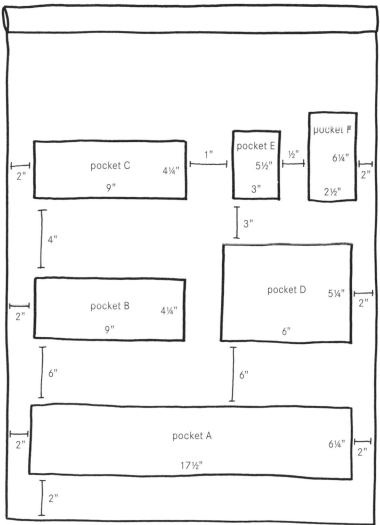

FIGURE **3**

CONTINUED

E. For pocket F. With the **Wrong** side of fabric facing up, fold one 3½" edge over ¼" toward the center of the pocket, then press. Fold over another ½" and press. Machine stitch a ⁵⁄₁₆" hem, making sure you stitch through all the layers. On the remaining three sides, with the **Wrong** side of the fabric facing up, fold over ¼" toward the center of the pocket, then press. Fold over another ¼" and press. Set aside.

STEP 3. stitch the pockets to the main panel of the wall organizer

With the **Right** sides facing up and using the illustration as a guide, pin the pockets to the main panel. Make sure the finished, stitched edge of each pocket is oriented toward the top edge of the main panel. Stitch each pocket in place, ⅛" from the outside edges of the pocket, along one side, across the bottom, then along the other side, backstitching at each end. Press. *see figure 3*

STEP 4. make smaller pocket slots

Lay the items you plan to stash in your wall organizer on top of each pocket. Use a ruler and a fadeout fabric marker to mark the stitching lines between the items. Be sure the lines are perpendicular to the bottom and parallel to each other. To finish the slots, stitch on each marked line, beginning at the bottom and stitching toward the top. Backstitch at each end.

STEP 5. make the rod casing

On each 6" side of the rod casing fabric, turn under ¼" toward the **Wrong** side and press, turn under another ¼" and press. Stitch down, using a ³⁄₁₆" seam allowance.

STEP 6. finish the wall organizer

A. Fold the rod casing in half with the two long sides lined up, **Wrong** sides together, and pin to the top edge of the organizer matching up the raw edges, using the illustration as a guide. With the **Right** sides together, pin the lining to the main panel, sandwiching the rod casing between the lining and the main panel. Stitch a ½" seam around all four sides, leaving a 5" opening on the bottom edge, backstitching at each end.

B. Using your scissors trim the corners at a 45-degree angle to reduce the bulk. (See page 140 for an explanation of mitering corners.)

C. Turn the wall organizer **Right**-side out. Use a point turner to push out the corners. (See page 141 for an explanation of a point turner.) To enclose the raw edges at the opening, fold them under ½" and pin the opening closed. Press. Then topstitch around all sides, ¼" in from the finished edge.

t o o l   r o l l

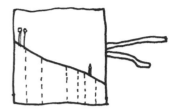

LEVEL 3

My own roll-up organizer is one of my favorite possessions. I use it for art supplies and carry it with me everywhere, but this design is suitable for organizing any kind of tools: knitting and sewing supplies, pencil collections, or a set of screwdrivers. The size and pockets can be customized to fit your specific organizational needs. This is a project to take on when you are fairly comfortable with your sewing machine, or as a challenge for the adventurous beginner.

FABRICS

¾ yard (44" wide) medium-weight cotton

1¼ yards (1" wide) twill tape

¾ yard (½" wide) twill tape

SUPPLIES

Yardstick

Fadeout fabric marker (or tailor's chalk)

Scissors

Straight pins

Ruler

notes

Preshrink fabric by washing, drying, and pressing before you start.

All seams are ½" unless otherwise stated. A ½" seam allowance is included in all cutting measurements.

CONTINUED

STEP 1. cut out all pieces from the fabric

Measure and mark the dimensions below directly onto the **Wrong** side of your fabric, using a yardstick and a fadeout fabric marker. Then, using your scissors, cut out each piece, following the marked lines.

From the fabric:
Cut 2 Tool Roll pieces (Interior and Exterior): 15½" wide x 17½" long

Cut 1 Pocket: 15½" wide; 5½" long on one side, 2" long on the other side. The top of the piece will be sloped as shown. *see figure 1*

From the 1" wide twill tape:
Cut 1 strip: 15¾" long

Cut 2 strips: 15" long

From the ½" wide twill tape:
Cut 1 strip: 24" long

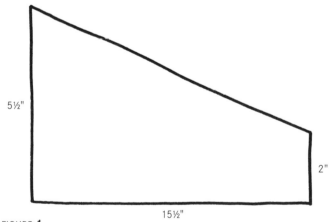

5½"

2"

15½"

FIGURE **1**

CONTINUED

STEP 2. make the tool roll

A. Fold the 15¾" piece of 1" wide strip of twill tape in half lengthwise and press. Place the sloped raw edge of the pocket inside the twill tape to enclose the raw edge, making sure the raw edge is butted up to the inside of the folded edge of the twill tape. Pin in place. Machine stitch close to the inside edge of the twill tape, making sure you stitch through all the layers.

B. With the **Right** sides of the interior and pocket piece facing up, pin the pocket along the bottom edge of the interior, matching up the raw edges of the sides and bottom. Beginning on the short side of the pocket, stitch a ¼" seam down the short side, across the bottom, and then back up the other side. Backstitch at each end.

C. Lay the craft tools you plan to stash in your tool roll on top of the pocket. Use a ruler and fadeout fabric marker to mark the stitching lines between the tools. Be sure the lines are perpendicular to the bottom and parallel to each other. To finish the tool slots, stitch on each marked line, beginning at the bottom and stitching toward the edge with the twill tape. Backstitch at each end. *see figure 2C*

D. With the **Wrong** side of the interior facing up, on the two 17½" long sides, fold over ½", then press. Set aside.

E. Take the 24" long piece of ½" twill tape and fold the short edges over ¼" and press. Fold over another ¼" and press. Stitch the folds in place, through all the layers, backstitching at each end. This will prevent the raw edges from unraveling. On the **Right** side of the exterior, pin the center of the length of twill tape to the piece, about 5" up from the bottom and ¾" in from the raw edge. Stitch the tape to the exterior piece, making a ½" square. *see figure 2E*

F. With the **Wrong** side of the exterior facing up, on the two 17½" long sides, fold over ½", then press.

STEP 3. finish the tool roll

A. Pin the interior (with the pocket) to the exterior, **Wrong** sides together, matching up the folded edges and the top and bottom raw edges. Stitch a ¼" seam down each long side, making sure you stitch through all the layers.

B. Fold both short edges of each 15" length of 1" wide twill tape over ¼", then press. Stitch the folds in place, through all the layers, backstitching at each end. This will prevent the raw edges from unraveling.

C. Next, fold each piece of twill tape in half lengthwise and press. Place the bottom raw edges of the tool roll inside one strip of twill tape to enclose it, making sure the raw edges are butted up to the folded edge of the twill tape. Pin in place. Stitch close to the inside of the twill tape, making sure you stitch through all the layers. Repeat this step with the top raw edges of the tool roll and the second strip of twill tape.

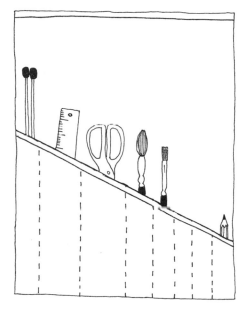

FIGURE **2C**

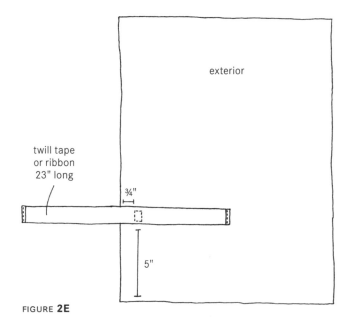

exterior

twill tape
or ribbon
23" long

¾"

5"

FIGURE **2E**

check book cover

FINISHED SIZE: 7" WIDE X 7¾" LONG WHEN OPENED FLAT

LEVEL 2

There is nothing charming about the checkbook covers your bank gives you. With a custom cover made out of beautiful hand-picked fabric, writing those checks becomes pure pleasure. Well . . . almost! The checkbook cover also makes a brilliant gift. This is a suitable sewing project for the beginner looking for a bit more of a challenge. Do not hesitate to experiment with different kinds of decorative trim and buttons on this little piece.

FABRICS

¼ yard (44" wide) medium-weight cotton

1 yard (½" wide) double-fold bias tape in coordinating or contrasting color

4" long (⅛" wide) piece elastic thread or cord

SUPPLIES

Yardstick

Fabric marker

Scissors

1 Button

Hand sewing needle and thread

Straight pins

notes

Preshrink fabric by washing, drying, and pressing before you start.

All seams are ½" unless otherwise stated. A ½" seam allowance is included in all cutting measurements and is marked on the pattern pieces.

CONTINUED

STEP 1. cut out all pieces from the fabric

Measure and mark the dimensions below directly onto the **Wrong** side of your fabric, using a yardstick and a fabric marker. Then, using your scissors, cut out each piece, following the marked lines.

From the fabric:
Cut 1 Cover: 7" wide x 7¾" long

Cut 2 Pockets: 3¾" wide x 7" long

From the double-fold bias tape:
Cut 1 piece 30" long

STEP 2. make the checkbook cover

A. With the **Wrong** side of one interior pocket facing up, on one 7" side, fold over ¼" toward the opposite side, and press. Fold over another ¼" and press. Machine stitch a ⅛" seam across the piece. Repeat this step with the other pocket. Set aside.

B. With the **Right** side of the checkbook cover fabric facing up, use your marker to make a small mark in the center of one 7" side, ¾" in from the edge. Center the button on the mark and sew in place using the hand sewing needle and thread.

C. With **Wrong** sides together, pin the unfinished 7" side of one pocket to a 7" side of the checkbook cover. Stitch a ¼" seam along the edge. Make sure you stitch through both layers of fabric. Repeat this step with the other pocket on the opposite side of the cover. Press. *see figure 2C*

STEP 3. finish the checkbook cover

A. With the **Right** side of the checkbook cover facing up, and the button closest to you, on the upper right corner, begin enclosing the edges of the checkbook cover in the 30" piece of bias tape. Make sure the raw end of the bias tape matches the raw edge of the 7" side opposite the side with the button and that the raw edge of the longer side of the checkbook cover is flush with the center fold of the bias tape. Pin in place.

B. To bind around the corner, fold the bias tape over itself creating a 45-degree mitered corner on both sides. Pin in place.

C. Continue sandwiching and pinning the binding in place, on the three remaining sides, mitering the next 2 corners. When you reach the corner where you started, fold the end of the bias tape under ½" so that the raw edge is tucked in. Pin in place. *see figure 3A+B+C*

D. Make a loop with the 4" piece of ⅛" wide elastic. With the exterior of the checkbook cover facing up, on the 7" side opposite the button, place the raw edges of the elastic loop under the bias tape, centering it. Pin in place. Stitch around all four sides, close to the inside edge of the bias tape. Make sure you stitch through all the layers, especially when turning and stitching corners. *see figure 3D*

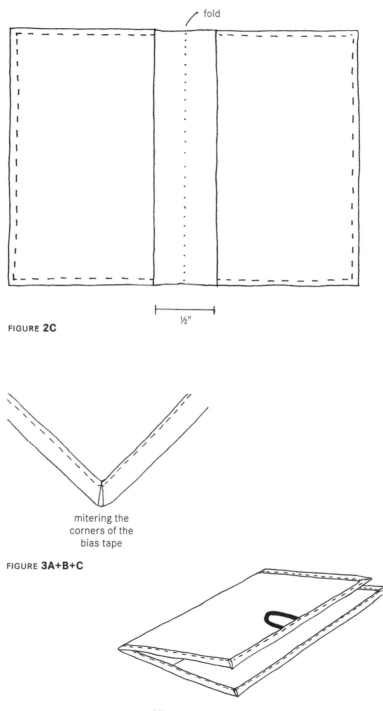

fold

½"

FIGURE **2C**

mitering the
corners of the
bias tape

FIGURE **3A+B+C**

FIGURE **3D**

bed pocket

FINISHED SIZE: TWIN (20" X 73"), QUEEN (20" X 94"), OR (KING 20" X 106")

LEVEL 2

The bed pocket is a splendid way to organize the clutter that builds up on the bedside table. Your books, magazines, hand lotion, and reading glasses all find a home in this easy and practical design. The bed pocket is a perfect beginner's project. It should be made out of a sturdy fabric. Note that the "wrong" side of the fabric shows on parts of the bed pocket, so choose a fabric that you like both sides of. If you can spend some more time with this project, why not add some appliqué?

FABRIC

Twin: 2⅞ yards medium-weight cotton

Queen: 3¼ yards medium-weight cotton

King: 3½ yards medium-weight cotton

SUPPLIES

Yardstick

Fabric marker

Scissors

Straight pins

Fadeout fabric marker (or tailor's chalk)

notes

Preshrink fabric by washing, drying, and pressing before you start.

All seams are ½" unless otherwise stated. A ½" seam allowance is included in all cutting measurements.

CONTINUED

STEP 1. cut out all pieces from the fabric

Measure and mark the dimensions below directly onto the **Wrong** side of your fabric, using a yardstick and a fabric marker. Then, using your scissors, cut out each piece, following the marked lines.

For a twin-size bed:
Cut 2 Main Panels: 21" wide x 46¾" long

Cut 2 Lining Panels: 21" wide x 37½" long

For a queen-size bed:
Cut 2 Main Panels: 21" wide x 57¼" long

Cut 2 Lining Panels: 21" wide x 48" long

For a king-size bed:
Cut 2 Main Panels: 21" wide x 63¼" long

Cut 2 Lining Panels: 21" wide x 54" long

STEP 2. make the main panel and pockets

A. With the **Wrong** side of one main panel piece facing up, fold one short edge over ¼" toward the center of the panel, then press. Fold over another ½" and press. Machine stitch a 5/16" seam, making sure you stitch through all the layers of fabric.

B. With the **Wrong** side still facing up, fold over another 9" and press. Pin in place. This will create one pocket.

C. Divide this pocket in half by marking a stitching line with a fadeout fabric marker down the center of the pocket, being sure that the line is perpendicular to the folded bottom edge and parallel to the sides. Stitch from the bottom of the pocket to the top, backstitching at each end. (You could, of course, make three or four divisions if you wish, depending on your needs!)

D. Repeat Steps 2A through 2C with the other main panel piece.

E. Lay the first main panel piece down with the pockets facing up. Place the second main panel piece over it, pockets down, with the **Right** side of the fabric facing up. Line up the raw 21" edges (without the pockets) of these two pieces and pin them together. Stitch together, backstitching at each end, then press the seam open. The **Wrong** side of the fabric is the **Right** side across the center of this project, but it will be hidden beneath your mattress! Your front panel should now measure 73" (twin), 94" (queen), or 106" (king) long. Set aside.

STEP 3. make the lining

A. With the **Right** sides of the lining pieces together, pin two of the 21" ends together, matching up the raw edges. Stitch together, backstitching at each end, then press the seam open.

B. With the **Wrong** side facing up, on one of the unstitched short side ends, fold over ¼" toward the center of the panel and press. Fold over another ¼" and press. Stitch a ³⁄₁₆" seam, backstitching at each end. Repeat with the opposite unstitched end. Your lining panel should now measure 73" (twin), 94" (queen), or 106" (king) long.

STEP 4. finish the bed pocket

A. With the **Right** side of the lining panel facing the pocket side of the main panel, pin the two pieces together, matching up the raw edges of the long sides, and making sure the pockets' raw edges are sandwiched between the two pieces. Also, make sure the short edges of the lining panel are matched up with the bottom, folded edge of the pockets. Stitch the panels together along one long side, backstitching at each end. Repeat with the other long side.

B. Turn the bed pocket **Right**-side out and press.

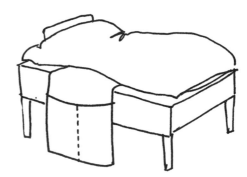

magazine holder

FINISHED SIZE: 11" WIDE X 20" TALL

LEVEL 3

Here is another great solution for organizing and keeping your magazines at hand. Of course this holder can hold other documents and important items as well, and even work for paper rolls in your bathroom or kitchen. This holder is good project for a beginner who is ready for the next step.

FABRICS

¾ yard (44" wide) canvas

SUPPLIES

Yardstick

Fabric marker

Scissors

Fadeout fabric marker (or tailor's chalk)

Wooden dowel (¾" or 1" diameter) (found at hardware or craft stores)

notes

Preshrink fabric by washing, drying, and pressing before you start.

All seams are ½" unless otherwise stated. A ½" seam allowance is included in all cutting measurements and is marked on the pattern pieces.

CONTINUED

STEP 1. cut out all pieces from the fabric

Measure and mark the dimensions below directly onto the **Wrong** side of your fabric, using a yardstick and a fabric marker. Then, using your scissors, cut out each piece, following the marked lines.

Cut 1 Backing: 12" wide x 24" long

Cut 1 Pocket: 8" wide x 28" long

STEP 2. make the backing

A. With the **Wrong** side of the backing facing up, on one 24" side, fold over ¼" toward the center of the backing, then press. Fold over another ¼" and press. Machine stitch in place a ³⁄₁₆" seam, backstitching at each end. Make sure you stitch through all the layers of fabric. Repeat with the other 24" side.

B. With the **Wrong** side of the backing facing up, on one 12" side, fold over ½" toward the center of the backing, then press. Fold over another 2" and press. Stitch in place using a 1⁷⁄₈" seam, backstitching at each end. Make sure you stitch through all the layers. This will be the top of the magazine holder. Fold bottom edge over ½" and press. Fold over another 1" and press. Stitch in place using a ⁷⁄₈" seam, backstitching at each end.

STEP 3. make the magazine pockets

A. With the **Wrong** side of the pocket facing up, on one 28" side, fold over ¼" toward the center of the pocket, and press. Fold over another ¼" and press. Stitch in place using a ³⁄₁₆" seam, backstitching at each end. Make sure you stitch through all the layers. Repeat with the other 28" side.

B. With the **Wrong** side of pocket facing up, on one 8" side, fold over ¼" toward the center of the pocket and press. Fold over another ¼ inch and press. Repeat on the second 8" side. Set aside.

STEP 4. finish the magazine holder

A. With the **Right** side of the pocket piece facing up, use a fadeout fabric marker and ruler to mark the stitching lines for the pockets 9" in from each edge, parallel with the 8" sides. You will have three 9" wide pockets.

B. With the **Right** side of the backing piece facing up, use a fadeout fabric marker and ruler to mark the stitching lines for placing the magazine pockets. Referring to the illustration, mark four stitching lines, parallel to the top and bottom edges. The first line should be placed ½" below seam for the rod casing, the second line 5" down from the first, the third 5" below that, and the fourth 5" below that, 2½" up from the bottom edge.

C. With the **Right** sides facing up, lay the pocket piece on top of the backing. Align the marked stitching lines of the pocket piece with the marked stitching lines of the backing piece. The top and bottom of the pocket will be stitched over the first and last stitching lines. Make sure to center the pocket piece on the backing piece (2" in from each side). Stitch the pocket piece to the backing piece, on the stitching lines.

D. Insert a dowel in the top hem (rod pocket) of the magazine holder.

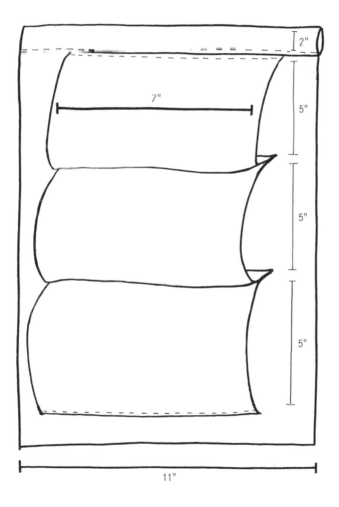

GLOSSARY AND TECHNIQUES

HAND APPLIQUÉ

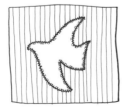

MACHINE APPLIQUÉ .

appliqué: A technique in which fabric shapes (motifs) are sewn on top of other pieces of fabric. You can apply them by hand or by using your sewing machine.

hand appliqué: Trace the motif on the wrong side of the fabric. Cut out the appliqué. Pin the appliqué in place. Machine stitch on the traced line. Cut around the appliqué ⅛" outside the stitching. Sew in place with an embroidery stitch.

machine appliqué: *Note that you will need a sewing machine with a zigzag option to machine appliqué.* Trace the motif on the wrong side of the fabric. Do NOT cut out the appliqué. Pin and baste the motif to background fabric. Machine stitch around the outline of the motif with a straight stitch. Then stitch over the straight stitch with a closely spaced zigzag stitch. Use small scissors to trim away fabric beyond the stitching.

backstitch: Backstitching prevents your seams from unraveling and gives added strength where it is needed, say, at the top of a pocket. Where specified, begin your seam normally for a few stitches, then put your sewing machine in "Reverse" and go back over the same stitches. Then sew forward again. Complete the seam and repeat the process at the opposite end if required.

baste: Basting is simply sewing using long, loose stitches to hold something in place temporarily. You can baste by hand or with the machine.

batting: Batting is loose fluffy filling material often used for lining quilts or to provide an insulating layer to a project. It can be made of cotton, wool, or synthetics and is available in a variety of forms at your local fabric store. Use the type specified where called for.

bias tape: Bias tape is available readymade at fabric stores. It is made from fabric strips cut on a 45-degree angle to the grain line. This bias cut creates an edging fabric that will stretch and flex to enclose smooth or curved edges.

clipping curves and corners: When a sewn piece has curves or angles you need to clip into the seam allowances to make the piece lie flat when it is turned right-side out. For corners, cut across the seam allowance at a 45-degree angle close to *but not into* the seam. For concave curves, like the inside of a C, simply make cuts perpendicular to the seam, coming close to the seam you've sewn but never through it. For convex curves, like the outside of a C, you will need to cut out little pie-shaped wedges to get rid of the excess bulk. Again, never cut through your seam.

cross stitch: *see hand embroidery*

fadeout marker: A fadeout marker can be found at fabric stores or hobby shops. It is a pen that will mark on fabric, but the marks will disappear in about 24 hours. This makes it very easy to use as you can mark the right or wrong side of the fabric. However, you will have to re-mark your fabric if you set it aside for too long!

grain: The grain is created in a woven fabric by the threads that travel lengthwise and crosswise. In a knitted fabric, the grain can be seen in the lengthwise ribs. Grain is always parallel to the selvedge edges.

grain lines: The direction of the grain. Often a pattern calls for matching the grain lines. Make sure the grain line marked on the pattern runs parallel to the grain of your fabric.

hand appliqué: *see appliqué*

hand embroidery: Hand embroidery designs are marked on the right side of the fabric. Try one of these stitches:

cross stitch: With tailor's chalk or a fadeout marker, make two parallel lines to mark the height of the stitch. Working from left to right, take diagonal stitches at even intervals between the lines with the needle pointed down. This makes the first half of the crosses. Then work from right to left and fill in the second half of the cross, keeping stitches even.

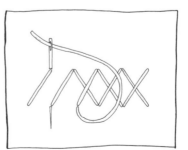

CROSS STITCH

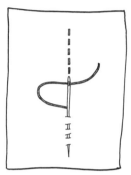

RUNNING STITCH

SATIN STITCH

running stitch: Working from left to right, make small even stitches. The stitch that shows should be the same width as the spaces between each stitch. As you gain experience, pick up several stitches on the needle and draw the thread through the fabric.

satin stitch: A series of parallel stitches worked closely together results in a decorative surface. This stitch can be used to fill in any outlined shapes.

hem: To hem is to finish the raw edge of something by folding it to the wrong side and sewing it in place. In this book, most hems are finished on the machine, but hemming is also done by hand. Follow the directions given within a pattern.

machine appliqué: *see appliqué*

miter: To join a seam at a 45-degree angle, like a picture frame. This gives a clean, professional-looking corner.

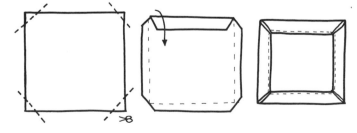

MITERING CORNERS

notches: Notches are small clips made in the seam allowance of a cut piece to use as a mark. Later, these notches will be matched up with other notches so your pieces will fit together just right. If you are squeamish about cutting into your seam, you might make a mark with your fabric marker instead.

point turner: When you have sewn something with a sharp corner, once you have clipped the excess fabric off at a 45-degree angle and turned the piece right-side out, you want to make sure that you've pushed the fabric all the way out to the corner. Your fingers are too big for the job. A point turner is a wooden or plastic tool with one pointed end and one rounded end made especially for the job and available in the notions section of a fabric store. You can also use a chopstick or knitting needle if you have one ready at hand.

preshrink: Many fabrics shrink when they are washed—and they do so at different rates! To spare yourself the heartache of having a finished piece ruined in the wash, shrink your fabrics before you use them. Simply wash, dry, and press all your fabrics as you will the finished item prior to getting started. Though you are tempted to get started with a project, don't skip this necessary first step!

raw edge: A raw edge is simply a cut edge before it is sewn or hemmed.

running stitch: *see hand embroidery*

satin stitch: *see hand embroidery*

seam allowance: The seam allowance is how much fabric there is between the raw edge and the seam. In this book, seam allowances are always figured in to the cutting dimensions so you don't have to add them in. Seam allowances are ¼" unless otherwise specified.

slip stitch: A slip stitch is a stitch that barely shows used in sewing together two finished (folded) edges. A slip stitch is made by running the needle inside the fold on one side, then picking up a few threads from the opposite side.

tailor's chalk: Tailor's chalk is found in the notions section of the fabric store. It can be used in the same places you would a fadeout marker. It's a little more old fashioned, but the chalk lines will last longer. When you've finished stitching, simply brush the chalk marks away.

topstitch: Topstitching is used both to hold pieces firmly in place and to add a slightly decorative edge. To topstitch, make a line of stitching on the outside of a piece, usually a set distance from an existing seam.

twill tape: A flat tape of woven ribbon made from cotton, linen, or other fabrics. It can be used as an edging material or to create things like hanging loops on towels.

RESOURCES

For some of the projects in this book I used fabric that I created and designed. You can buy my fabric by the yard and also buttons and ribbon on my Web site. Please visit me online at www.jansdotter.com.

shop

AMERICAN SCIENCE SURPLUS
www.sciplus.com
This is where we ordered the glass test tubes for the Curtain with Pockets project. You can play around with different sizes of the test tubes for the pockets, but we recommend going with 20 x 150 mm.

AMY BUTLER DESIGNS
www.amybutlerdesign.com
My friend Amy Butler, who's based in Ohio, designs colorful and inspiring fabrics. Visit her Web site and search under "where to buy" to find retailers near you that carry her fabrics.

B&J FABRICS
wwwbandjfabrics.com
This family-owned fabric store in Manhattan has a remarkable selection of beautiful fabrics. Their inventory will make you swoon. If you're into sewing, the wonderfully helpful and knowledgeable staff plus amazing selection make it the place to shop.

BRITEX FABRICS
www.britexfabrics.com
Britex is a landmark destination in San Francisco for anybody who loves fabrics and notions. They have a very knowledgeable staff and four floors packed with a great selection. If you don't live in the Bay Area, use their mail order form online.

CONTEMPORARY CLOTH
www.contemporarycloth.com
This online fabric store has many different kinds of contemporary motifs and designs on fabric. Search their online catalog by designer or style.

CREATE FOR LESS
www.createforless.com
Create for Less sells more than 50,000 brand-name craft supplies at wholesale prices and in bulk quantities. Search by brand, holiday, season, theme, occasion, or craft type—you're bound to find the notions you need here.

DENVER FABRICS
www.denverfabrics.com
This supply store sells notions and fabric at discount prices. Shop online or visit their stores in Denver and Littleton, CO.

DISCOUNT FABRICS
www.discountfabrics-sf.com
Discount Fabrics carries remnants, leftover fabric, and short runs. It's pretty budget friendly and you can find some really good deals if you dig around a little. And it is a great source for cheap muslin and canvas. They have three locations in San Francisco.

HANCOCK FABRICS
www.hancockfabrics.com
Hancock Fabrics is America's largest fabric store. Need I say more?

MELINAMADE
www.melinamade.com
Here you'll find vintage-inspired patterns that are hand-printed on barkcloth fabric. It's hard not to get distracted by their neat wallpapers!

M&J TRIMMING
www.mjtrim.com
M&J stocks almost everything you might need in trims: ribbons, elastic tape, buttons, and tassels. It never ends . . . they have an amazing array of choices. If you cannot visit their store in NYC, shop online.

MOOD FABRICS
www.moodfabrics.com
Yes, it is true . . . Mood really is amazing. Not only do they have an endless amount of fabrics and so many, many different choices, their staff is also very friendly and helpful. This is simply a "must visit" when you're in NYC. Last time I spent four hours there—honest truth.

POPPY FABRICS
www.poppyfabric.com
Poppy Fabrics is another favorite fabric store of mine. They have a lot of European fabrics and an interesting collection of dress and vinyl-coated fabrics. And a great home décor department, too!

REPRODEPOT FABRICS
www.reprodepotfabrics.com
Reprodepot Fabrics has the best selection of reproduction fabrics. The prints are so fun and inspiring and sold at very good prices. This company is owned and run by one really nice lady . . . support her online.

RIBBON JAR
www.ribbonjar.com
A cute online store that offers all kinds of ribbons and trims. They share some projects ideas, too!

SEWING MACHINES PLUS
www.sewingmachinesplus.com
Go online to purchase needles, thread, embroidery supplies, and, you guessed it, sewing machines from this family-owned business.

STITCH LOUNGE
www.stitchlounge.com
This is a really brilliant place in San Francisco's Hayes Valley neighborhood. Their fabrics, both vintage and contemporary, are limited but well chosen. And everything's affordable. You can also rent studio time or take classes.

TEXTILE ARTS
www.txtlart.com
Yes, you *can* buy Marimekko and Ljungbergs textiles online in America. These Scandinavian companies make bold and incredible fabrics that remain timeless year after year. I strongly recommend you visit this Web site and invest in a yard of classic designer fabric.

TWENTY2
www.twenty2.net
Twenty2 sells modern, retro-inspired, and simply great fabrics that are created by a husband-and-wife team in Brooklyn, NY (available for sale at their showroom or online).

read

www.craftlog.org
When entering this Web site, beware: you can lose hours browsing the best links, tips, and inspiration. Search for "textiles" or "sewing" and a whole world opens up to you!

www.fitnyc.edu
The Fashion Institute of Technology (FIT) is a great school and has a great site. The school also has a museum in NYC that is free to visit!

www.kitty-craft.com
Kitty Craft is cutesy, cutesy Japanese style. They sell many different kinds of sweet fabrics but the site has *so* much more . . . ideas, inspiration, and books.

Reader's Digest Complete Guide to Sewing
This is an incredible book that covers everything you need to know about basic sewing.

www.selvedge.org
My favorite reading about "everything textiles" is a British magazine called *Selvedge. Selvedge* offers the world's finest textile photography, unparalleled design, and peerless writing—it is simply fabulous and so inspiring! There is nothing like it.

www.textilesociety.org
The Textile Society of America's site has endless listings of links and workshops you might find useful.

www.textilesociety.org.uk
If you like the Textile Society of America's site, then visit the British version where you'll find even more information! So much to do, see, and make . . . so little time!

www.twistedthread.com
This is a British site that lists different trade shows and exhibitions for people who love to sew, stitch, and embroider. Who knows . . . you might go one day! I am considering it.

INDEX

A
acrylics, 16
appliqué, 138
aprons
    cafe, with pocket, 31–33
    reversible, 44–49

B
backpack, simple
        drawstring, 83–87
backstitching, 138
basting, 138
batting, 139
bed pocket, 131–33
bias tape, 139

C
cafe apron with pocket, 31–33
checkbook cover, 127–29
chopstick pocket, placemats
        with, 21–23
coasters, 24
corners
    clipping, 139
    mitering, 140
cotton, 15
covers
    checkbook, 127–29
    duvet, 94–99
cross stitch, 139
curtain with pockets, 91–93
curves, clipping, 139

D
doorstop, 108–13
draft snake, 105–7
duvet cover, 94–99

E
embellishments, 17
embroidery, hand, 139–40
equipment, 13

F
fabrics
    combining, 17
    flammable, 16
    kinds of, 15–16
    preshrinking, 141
    reusing, 15
    shopping for, 142–43
fadeout marker, 139

G
gardening tote, 61–66
grain, 139
grain lines, 139

H
hand appliqué, 138
hand embroidery, 139–40
hat, sun, 77–81
hems, 140

K
kitchen towels, 41–43

L
linen, 15

M
machine appliqué, 138
magazine holder, 134–37
mitering, 140

N
napkins, 24–26
notches, 141
nylon, 16

O
oven mitt, 34–39

P
picnic placemat, 51–53
pillowcase, 101–3
placemats
    with chopstick pocket, 21–23
    picnic, 51–53
point turner, 141
pot holder, 27–29
preshrinking, 141

R
raw edge, 141
rayon, 16
reversible apron, 44–49
running stitch, 140

S
satin stitch, 140
seam allowance, 141
shopping, 142–43
slip stitch, 141
snake, draft, 105–7
stitches
    back-, 138
    cross, 139
    running, 140
    satin, 140
    slip, 141
    top-, 141
sun hat, 77–81

T
tailor's chalk, 141
techniques, 138–41
tool roll, 121–25
topstitching, 141
tote bags
    all-day, 71–76
    gardening, 61–66
    simple, 56–60
towels, kitchen, 41–43
twill tape, 141

W
wall organizer, 117–20
Web sites, 142–43
wool, 16

Y
yoga mat tote, 67–70

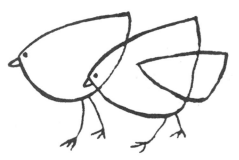